THE VOLUNTEER TREASURER'S HANDBOOK
FINANCIAL MANAGEMENT BUILDING BLOCKS
FOR NOT-FOR-PROFIT ORGANIZATIONS
By Howard B. Levy, CPA

Here's what readers are saying about this HANDBOOK:

THE VOLUNTEER TREASURER'S HANDBOOK

FINANCIAL MANAGEMENT BUILDING BLOCKS FOR NOT-FOR-PROFIT ORGANIZATIONS

By **Howard B. Levy, CPA**

PIERCY, BOWLER, TAYLOR & KERN

Certified Public Accountants & Business Advisors
A Professional Corporation

6100 Elton Ave., Suite 1000
Las Vegas, Nevada 89107

THE VOLUNTEER TREASURER'S HANDBOOK

FINANCIAL MANAGEMENT BUILDING BLOCKS FOR NOT-FOR-PROFIT ORGANIZATIONS

By **Howard B. Levy, CPA**

LIBRARY OF CONGRESS CATALOG CARD NUMBER: 99-91134

ISBN 0-9674896-0-1 19.95

PUBLISHED BY *PIERCY, BOWLER, TAYLOR & KERN*

Certified Public Accountants & Business Advisors
A Professional Corporation

6100 Elton Ave., Suite 1000
Las Vegas, Nevada 89107

Tel. 702/384-1120
Fax 702/870-2474
e-mail pbtk@pbtk.com
www.pbtk.com

Cover design by Jerry Presnell, **Image Designers**, Apopka, Florida
Printed and bound in the United States of America
    by **Creel Printing Co.**, Las Vegas, Nevada

THE VOLUNTEER TREASURER'S HANDBOOK

FINANCIAL MANAGEMENT BUILDING BLOCKS
FOR NOT-FOR-PROFIT ORGANIZATIONS

ABOUT THE AUTHOR:

Howard B. Levy, CPA, has provided professional accounting, auditing and financial management consulting services and worked with officers, board members and executives of not-for-profit organizations, for more than 25 years. In either a professional capacity, or that of a volunteer, he has helped them to identify financial management needs and objectives, to select and prioritize ways to achieve those objectives, and to instill among those who provide and receive the organization's support (including donors, program beneficiaries, and concerned regulators) confidence and trust in their commitment to fiscal integrity and responsible leadership.

Mr. Levy was the 1993-1994 Chairman of the Florida Institute of Certified Public Accountants' Not-for-Profit Organizations Committee. He is a member of the National Center for Nonprofit Boards, and from 1987 to 1994, was national Treasurer and Chief Financial Officer of The Amyotrophic Lateral Sclerosis (ALS) Association, an organization dedicated to finding the cause and cure of "Lou Gehrig's Disease." This **HANDBOOK** is derived in large part from material originally developed by Mr. Levy to guide the volunteer treasurers of The ALS Association's network of local chapters throughout the United States.

Mr. Levy is currently a principal and Director of Quality Control Services for *PIERCY, BOWLER, TAYLOR AND KERN* (www.pbtk.com), a leading local firm of certified public accountants serving the not-for-profit, governmental and business communities in Las Vegas, Nevada. He also provides consulting services to other CPAs around the nation in the not-for-profit and other professional practice areas. Until 1990, Mr. Levy served for seven years as the accounting and auditing quality control partner of a large, international firm of CPAs. He is also a former member of the American Institute of Certified Public Accountants' two most senior professional standards-setting bodies, its Accounting Standards Executive Committee and Auditing Standards Board. Previously, he was Adjunct Assistant Professor of Accounting at Dowling College, in Oakdale, New York.

You can contact Mr. Levy at hlevy@pbtk.com.

Photo by Burton Studio, Las Vegas, Nevada

THE VOLUNTEER TREASURER'S HANDBOOK

FINANCIAL MANAGEMENT BUILDING BLOCKS
FOR NOT-FOR-PROFIT ORGANIZATIONS

By **Howard B. Levy, CPA**

ACKNOWLEDGMENTS:

The author gratefully thanks the other principals of the firm of *PIERCY, BOWLER, TAYLOR & KERN* for their long-standing and continuing commitment and support for volunteerism and the not-for-profit community and for allowing him the opportunity to complete this work. He particularly acknowledges the contribution of Richard H. Bowler, CPA, one of the firm's founding principals and shareholders, and its not-for-profit practice leader, and the following other associates, colleagues and friends who reviewed and commented upon all or part of the manuscript:

- Errol Copilevitz, Esq., Shareholder
  Copilevitz & Canter, LLC, Attorneys, Kansas City, MO

- Michael W. Havlicek, national President and Chief Executive Officer and
  Benjamin S. Ohrenstein, Esq., CPA, national Treasurer and Chief Financial Officer
  The Amyotrophic Lateral Sclerosis Association, Calabasas Hills, CA

- Roger A. Rolfe, Certified Investment Management Analyst and Senior Vice President
  Morgan Stanley Dean Witter, Clearwater, FL

- Susan D. Schubert (Trainer, Speaker, Facilitator)
  Schubert-Kravitz Associates, Pickerington, OH

- Charles Selcer, CPA, Shareholder
  Schechter Dokken Kanter Andrews & Selcer Ltd., CPAs, Minneapolis, MN

- Stephen Webb, Senior Pension Consultant
  Lebenson Actuarial Services, Inc., Las Vegas, NV

- Garth R. Winckler, President and Chief Professional Officer
  United Way of Southern Nevada, Las Vegas, NV

The author also acknowledges and thanks the trustees of the ALS Association for giving him the opportunity to serve as its national treasurer for seven years, which this author believes is the most important thing he has ever done and which he found to be a most rewarding experience.

THE VOLUNTEER TREASURER'S HANDBOOK

FINANCIAL MANAGEMENT BUILDING BLOCKS FOR NOT-FOR-PROFIT ORGANIZATIONS

By **Howard B. Levy, CPA**

TABLE OF CONTENTS

TABLE OF CONTENTS (continued)

PAGE

INTRODUCTION

If you are the treasurer of a not-for-profit organization, ask yourself:

* Does your organization *know where it wants to be* in five years, and does it have a *plan* to get there?

* Is your organization preparing and using its budget as *an effective planning* tool — and a *control* device?

* Does the Board effectively meet its *financial oversight* responsibility?

* Does the organization have adequate controls over the approval and processing of transactions and efficient, productive use of its resources?

* What happened at United Way in 1992 — and how is it affecting your organization today?

If you're not sure your answers to these or similar questions are the right answers — *then read on!*

What happened at United Way? Near the dawn of this decade, United Way of America (UWA) found itself at the heart of a financial scandal ranking closely behind that of the savings and loan industry in piquing the outrage of the American public. UWA's chief executive, William Aramony was fired in March 1992 from his $400,000-a-year+ position after discovery of a pattern of reckless spending on luxury travel and other perks, and engaging in questionable, self-serving transactions of significance, over the 22-year period of his leadership. In legal pleadings responding to a lawsuit from Aramony (seeking payment of his pension benefits and still unresolved in 1999), UWA claimed total lost revenues ranging from $16 to $37 million for it and its 1,400 local affiliates because of the adverse publicity following discovery of the matter. Aramony was convicted of fraud in 1995 and is now serving time on a 6½-year sentence.

The American public has always been suspicious of perceived high salaries and other "wastes and excesses" of those who manage charitable and other not-for-profit organizations, particularly larger ones — and many often cite this as a reason not to give. Americans have never understood the impossibility of conducting the kinds of grand, noble and essential programs that our charities do, without talented, well trained and dedicated people, people who forego opportunities to use their knowledge and skills more lucratively elsewhere — not for one or two nights a month and an occasional weekend as a volunteer — but for their whole careers, their lives. These are people who, for the most part, need and deserve a decent livelihood and a comfortable work environment. Yes, our charities need to compete aggressively, not just with other charities as they do for donors' dollars, but with private industry (and government) for these talented people with vision, ideals and dedication. But every now and then, along comes a bad apple (or a good apple turns rotten) like the now infamous William Aramony.

Based on its 9-week investigation, in April 1992, a Washington DC law firm issued a 59-page report to United Way's Board of Governors, in which it described the affair as "a story of excesses and lost values," characterized it as a "breach of trust" and blamed it principally on the "looseness and independence of Mr. Aramony's management style over the course of more than two decades." However, the substantial excesses, abuses and mistakes (to be charitable), described in detail in the report (and probably only the "tip of the iceberg") cannot be blamed only on one man and his "management style." The fault rests squarely with UWA's Rip Van Winkle board, whose misplaced trust went unchallenged for over twenty years, and who permitted this independent "management style" to go on that long, a situation wholly inconsistent with its fiduciary responsibilities as a governing board. And where was its treasurer? It is more than a story of excesses and lost values; it is a story of abdication of responsibility.

The diminution of public trust that United Way felt reverberated loudly and quickly throughout the not-for-profit world. All over the nation, newspapers reported that, in the aftermath of the scandal, charities who depended on allocations from local United Way agencies were scrambling for new funding sources to cover reductions in the allocations expected to result from the scandal. They feared that the United Way agencies could no longer raise enough money to meet their needs. Those that employed professional staff braced themselves to reduce their support as a direct result of anticipated public criticism of executive salaries and expenses, which, no matter how fair and reasonable they might be for the services received, were expected to be perceived as excessive by the uninformed. But criticism from the uninformed (especially those looking for an excuse to withhold contributions) is something the nation's charities can do little about; they can't be diverting significant resources from important programs to teach the public the realities of not-for-profit management.

When the UWA story broke in 1992, the editor and publisher of *THE NONPROFIT BOARD REPORT*, Larry Sterne, wrote, "The board's failure to exercise sufficient oversight over finances, and its failure to appreciate the extent of donors' concerns over such issues, makes a perfect case study for other trustees around the country." Sterne went on to admonish present and prospective board members not to agree to serve "...unless you fully appreciate your fiduciary responsibility..." and not to "...give up your authority as a board member just because the leader may be popular or charismatic."

Yes, the United Way "debacle" (as it was termed in the press) was about board responsibility and control. And the best recommendation for all charities, small and large, is to make a self evaluation — *NOW* — if not done already, of the extent of involvement and control exercised by your governing board, not just in regard to major transactions and events, but in the day-to-day management of the organization, and to take all steps necessary to correct any weaknesses before anyone can criticize your operation.

Just as we are in the "post-Watergate" era in politics, in the not-for-profit world we are in the "post-Aramony" era. The impact of the Aramony legacy continues to be felt by all charities, even the smallest ones that employ only volunteers. More than ever, public charities find themselves in a fishbowl — ***and it had better not smell fishy!*** Perhaps as part of the UWA aftermath, the Internal Revenue Service has been empowered to impose sanctions with regard to executive compensation and conflicts of interest (see chapter 14). Heightened scrutiny comes not just from the unfounded criticisms of the uninformed, but from regulators and "watchdog" organizations groups, operating on behalf of the donating public, on all charities — just because of a few rotten apples (or rotten fish).

Because of the 1992 UWA scandal, governing boards of charities can continue to expect to be called to task in various ways to demonstrate that they are meeting their responsibilities — and they had better be ready for this challenge. If the United Way tragedy should have taught us one thing, it should be not just to control the salaries, "perks" and expenses of key executives, it is that trust must be continually earned, not taken for granted — not only the trust placed by the board in its key management people, but the trust placed by the public in the board, no matter how prestigious its membership roster.

What are not-for-profit organizations? We use the term "not-for-profit" (or "nonprofit") to describe philanthropic, charitable or social welfare institutions and other organizations that enhance the fabric of American society, and are (a) neither business (often called "for-profit") nor government, and (b) often managed and staffed mostly by volunteers. According to the Financial Accounting Standards Board (see chapter 3), "not-for-profit organization" is defined as:

> An entity that possesses the following characteristics [in varying degrees] that distinguish it from a business enterprise: (a) contributions of significant amounts of resources from resource providers who do not expect commensurate or proportionate pecuniary return, (b) operating purposes other than to provide goods or services at a profit, and (c) absence of ownership interests like those of business enterprises.

According to "What You Should Know About Nonprofits," a joint publication of the National Center for Nonprofit Boards and INDEPENDENT SECTOR (two not-for-profit organizations.):

> The nonprofit sector in the United States is vast and diverse and touches all our lives. It includes more than a million organizations that spend nearly $500 billion each year more than the gross domestic product of Brazil, Russia, or Australia. About six percent of all organizations in the U.S. are nonprofits, and one in 15 Americans works for a nonprofit. Within this disparate group are many types of organizations. Section 501(c) of the tax code, which outlines the types of organizations eligible for tax exemption, lists more than 25 classifications of nonprofits.*

Examples of not-for-profit organizations include, among others, the following types of nongovernmental organizations:

---

* The full text of "What You Should Know About Nonprofits" is available at www.ncnb.org.

- Cemetery societies
- Civic and community associations
- Colleges and universities
- Elementary and secondary schools
- Federated fund-raising organizations
- Fraternal organizations
- Labor unions
- Libraries
- Museums
- Performing arts organizations
- Political parties
- Political action committees
- Private and community foundations
- Professional associations
- Public broadcasting stations
- Religious organizations
- Research and scientific organizations
- Social and country clubs
- Trade associations
- Voluntary health and welfare organizations
- Zoological and botanical societies

The terms "not-for-profit" and "nonprofit" do not mean that these organizations cannot or should not charge fees for goods or services provided or generate profits (revenues in excess of expenses); it means that, unlike businesses, their purpose is not to earn money for owners or other investors but to provide some needed social benefit for some segment of society. Often, the achievement of the mission or purpose of a not-for-profit organization is directly and critically dependent upon its ability to raise, accumulate and manage its financial resources. Accumulating financial resources over time require that an entity not spend all its revenues currently — in essence, maintain profitable operations. In fact, many not-for-profit organizations engage in business activities in competition with for-profit enterprises.

About this HANDBOOK. This **HANDBOOK** was prepared primarily to help volunteer treasurers (of local, regional and small national charities and other not-for-profit organizations) do their jobs better. However, while it speaks directly to treasurers, reading it would benefit board chairpersons, presidents, all finance, budget, investment, and audit committee members and selected staff. Your attention is particularly directed to the "key thoughts," which appear in italics and are set off from the rest of the text with key symbols, as follows: "*key thought*."

This **HANDBOOK** is a brief summary of many fundamental principles of financial management, as they apply to typical local not-for-profit organizations (including chapters or other affiliates of larger organizations) — principles that every treasurer should know something about — and presented in clear, non-technical, concise, and *practical* terms. Therefore, it is readable. It does not purport to cover any of these topics in an exhaustive or even comprehensive fashion. The subject matter of virtually any chapter can fill (and has filled) volumes by itself.

This **HANDBOOK** is *not an accounting textbook* — and it will *not* make an accountant — or even a bookkeeper — out of the untrained and inexperienced. It will not eliminate the need for expert advice on the application of generally accepted accounting principles or how to complete required government forms or for bookkeeping training or assistance from someone experienced. It will not necessarily answer all your questions or address all your concerns. But it will help you, as the treasurer, and others involved in financial management and reporting, to understand and meet your critical responsibilities to perform or oversee your organization's accounting and other financial management functions effectively and — possibly most importantly — help you determine *when to ask for help*. Your efforts will go a long way in maximizing the trust placed in your organization by its constituents.

Operating efficiencies may be obtained by delegating certain board responsibilities to board committees, such as executive committees, audit committees or finance committees. Although delegation enables boards to divide their agendas among the smaller, working committees and achieve more in less time, it does not mean abdication. Of course, when it comes to financial management, the treasurer is the lead player (see chapter 1). But even when using committees to do most of the work, the board must exercise an oversight responsibility, and monitor the work of the committees, to assure itself that the committee's, the board's — and the organization's — objectives are met.

If your organization's board is made up largely of respected community leaders who provide financial support and the prestige of their names, but have neither the time nor the inclination to take their fiduciary

6

responsibilities as board members seriously (like UWA's before 1992), consider whether these people should serve, instead, on some honorary board, without such responsibilities, and be replaced on the governing board by others who will provide the necessary involvement and control. ↤

In meeting their fiduciary oversight responsibilities, the board, or a designated committee thereof — and the treasurer, in particular — must have significant familiarity and involvement with the budgeting and financial reporting process, and with other internal controls, policies and procedures. It doesn't matter how much of the related duties are performed by paid executives and staff — or how talented they are. When independent auditors are employed, they must have regular meetings, at least annually, with the board or an appropriate financial oversight committee thereof. Board members meet with auditors to gain an understanding of the audit objectives, approach and findings and to assure that the auditors have an understanding of the board's objectives and concerns in conducting the audit.

↦*It is of primary importance for board members exercising the financial oversight role to maintain an attitude of independent, objective evaluation — even a healthy skepticism.* ↤ It is not appropriate to accept — and "rubber stamp" — everything management leaders do and say, merely because you respect them as highly trained, experienced professionals, because you believe them to have the highest integrity, because they are more knowledgeable, in many respects, than most board members, or because everything seems to be going well. Ask the hard questions, and consider the answers critically, cautiously and responsibly.

If this is not your board's "style" — and your style, as treasurer — your organization might very well find itself in a "fine kettle of fish" — like United Way of America did. Don't let your organization's board wait 22 years for its wake-up call —like United Way did. It might come sooner — **and louder** — than you think.

↦*Please **do not** allow yourself to be overwhelmed with the need for change. While the financial management recommendations that follow are all important, they need not be implemented all at once. View them as goals to be achieved over a reasonable period of time —like building blocks.* ↤ Work with your finance or audit committee to prioritize your goals and develop a program and timetable to help keep you on target.

CHAPTER 1: ROLE OF THE TREASURER

↪*Money is your only weapon, other than the dedication of your volunteers and staff, to enable your organization to achieve its mission, whatever that is. If you ever want to achieve your mission, you must manage your precious little money the best you can to get the most out of it.*↩ Therefore, as in any other volunteer organization, the treasurer's role is not only central; in a word, it is *vital*.

As discussed in the introduction to this **HANDBOOK,** the 1990s have brought a hotbed of activity directed at the not-for-profit sector — fueled early in the decade by the United Way/William Aramony scandal and a series of exposés in the Philadelphia Inquirer — by media, public "watchdog" organizations and government (including the Internal Revenue Service and the United States Congress). The objective of all this activity has been to focus critical attention on, and demand improvements in, fiscal accountability among not-for-profit organizations.

Coincidentally, perhaps, decades of heated controversy over financial accounting principles applicable to not-for-profit organizations have culminated over the last five years in new standards that have required sweeping changes in the look of their financial statements and related disclosures. And it has not ended yet.

Accountability, it seems therefore, has been the principal message to be heeded by members of our nation's volunteer sector to assure their continued success as we move into the next millenium.

Since the treasurer, the board and the board committees function as fiduciaries, they are responsible for the funds entrusted to them by donors. However, they are also volunteers who can devote only limited time to meeting these responsibilities.

↪*As treasurer, you are the organization's chief financial officer and are charged with effectively planning, organizing, coordinating, directing, controlling, recording and reporting the financial activities of your organization, and safeguarding its resources for judicious use in accordance with its purpose.*↩ Like any other officer or trustee, your responsibility is that of a fiduciary. But you are *primarily* responsible for the organization's financial accountability.

Among other things, the treasurer is usually responsible for compliance with federal, state and, sometimes, local reporting requirements (see chapter 12), established policies and procedures of your organization's board of trustees or directors and those of any affiliated central organization, and for liaison with its independent accountants (see chapter 10). Accordingly, you will ordinarily chair a finance or similar committee made up of other trustees who will assist you in meeting some of these responsibilities. (In smaller organizations, however, you will *be* the finance committee.)

As part of your responsibility for safeguarding resources, you are often responsible, also, to assess the organization's insurance needs periodically. Most jurisdictions afford some statutory shelter or limited immunity ("safe harbor," if you will) from liability for board members, including enabling the organization to legally indemnify directors for any expense or liability incurred as a result of performing the duties of a director provided they act in good faith in the interests of the organization. Often, the law permits indemnification only in certain circumstances and may require either a provision in the organization's by-laws or an agreement with directors. *Because of potentially significant limitations inherent in this protection, however, directors and officers (D&O) liability insurance is frequently a wise investment since it is effective in circumstances not shielded under the law.* Also, in addition to protecting the directors from liability, D&O insurance will provide funds to reimburse the organization for expenditures made or incurred to directors under indemnification provisions. Because inherent risks associated with this type of coverage are different from those of commercial enterprises, only a policy designed specifically for not-for-profit organizations should be purchased, usually from an agency that specializes therein (see the last paragraph of Chapter 16).

Other forms of insurance that need to be considered, based on the organization's operations and other circumstances, include general liability, fire and theft and, if there are employees, employee honesty surety bonds, workers' compensation, and health and other employee benefits (see chapter 14).

It can be said that any organization is only as healthy as its financial condition and the quality of its financial management. As treasurer, your goal should be to provide sound financial management and the leadership needed to set the proper tone for fiscal integrity and responsibility. In doing so, you will help your organization instill trust and confidence among its many constituencies who provide — and receive — its support, including donors, program beneficiaries and concerned regulators acting in the public interest.

Accordingly, the treasurer holds one of the most demanding and important leadership positions in any not-for-profit organization. To do it right, the treasurer's job requires time, a certain amount of knowledge and talent, and a lot of dedication. But if you read and follow the guidance set forth in the succeeding chapters, you should be able easily to meet your formidable responsibilities, perhaps with the aid of other volunteers and professionals, and achieve your goal.

Good Luck!

CHAPTER 2: INTERNAL CONTROL

As any accountant will tell you, the very foundation of management's stewardship function, the essence of sound financial management and fiscal responsibility for any organization, whether for-profit or not, is its internal control, and the chief financial officer (ordinarily, the treasurer in a not-for-profit) is at its cornerstone.

Unfortunately, many who manage not-for-profit organizations, particularly smaller ones, often staffed solely by volunteers, do not consider internal control important, partly because of the organization's smallness, and its inability to segregate duties, and partly because a system of checks and balances is seen by some as an unbefitting indication of lack of trust.

It is true that the most important element of internal control in any volunteer organization, no matter how large or small, is the integrity of its volunteers (and staff, if any) and their dedication to the organization's altruistic cause. *But it is foolish, indeed, to rely solely on that integrity and dedication when there are any number of prudent control procedures that may be implemented at little or no cost, and that would provide reasonable assurance to donors (and regulators who protect them) that management is worthy of the public trust placed in it — even when segregation of duties is impossible.*

Among others, the principal overall objectives of internal control for any not-for-profit organization are:

- To provide management with reasonable assurance about the reliability of the financial reporting process, and

- To safeguard the organization's resources and provide reasonable assurance that they are used in accordance with management's authorization, any applicable donor restrictions and the organization's purpose and functional budgetary goals.

These objectives are not related solely to protection from misappropriation or defalcation (fraud) — something you would like to think is extremely rare in organizations with such noble purposes and dedicated volunteers as yours. They relate to an even greater extent to assuring the achievement of the organization's mission and objectives and protection from the effects of inadvertent human error — something we all are, unfortunately, far more prone to.

The term *"reasonable assurance"* is key here because it is generally too expensive and thus, counterproductive, to provide absolute assurance. All internal control policies and procedures must be practical in the circumstances; they must be cost effective to achieve the objective of adequately safeguarding an entity's resources. (You wouldn't pay a $100 insurance premium to protect a piece of jewelry that is worth $75, would you?) Consequently, we develop controls that can be relied on, at reasonable cost, to prevent or detect not *all* errors or improprieties, but only those that have both a reasonable probability of occurrence and are potentially significant or material.

The objectives we spoke of are, of course, quite general. ↦*However, to design and select internal control policies and procedures that are practical and cost effective, one needs to focus on **specific** control objectives — and the risks that make them important, in specific areas of concern. Control objectives can be achieved even when segregation of duties is not cost-effective and, therefore, impractical, by selecting reasonably effective control policies and procedures that are responsive to the identified risks. Those control policies and procedures that are unnecessary, because they are either irrelevant to the risks, redundant or otherwise ineffective, can be avoided so as to manage the costs of control.* ↤

Some examples of key control objectives — together with related control policies and procedures (discussed in further detail in the chapters that follow) typically used to address them — are that:

- **Financial statements** (see chapter 3) are timely, accurate and complete — prepared or reviewed by treasurer, well designed books of account with appropriate chart of accounts, and tailored financial statement software with restricted access thereto (physical locks, confidential computer codes), data input/output controls, backup files (see chapter 15)

- **Cash disbursements** are properly authorized and expenses properly classified and allocated functionally — budgets prepared with extensive board involvement and variance analysis procedures (see chapter 4) (see chapter 4), dual signatures, required written approvals, documented support, time recording procedures, cancellations and internal audit procedures, for example, regarding invoices and employee time and expense reports, timely bank reconciliations prepared or reviewed by the treasurer, numerical accountability and physical controls over unused checks (see chapter 7)

- **Cash receipts** (see chapter 5) are properly recorded and deposited — mail opening procedures, segregation of duties with donor restrictions properly identified, complied with and accounted for

- **Donor database** records (see chapter 6) are adequately safeguarded — physical locks, confidential computer access codes, input/output controls, backup files

- **Movable property assets** (for example, computer equipment) are properly recorded in accordance with organization's capitalization policy, depreciated and controlled — periodic asset inventory and tagging procedure.

CHAPTER 3: ACCOUNTING AND FINANCIAL REPORTING

If internal control is the foundation of sound financial management, the accounting and financial reporting process is its main structure.

↪*Accounting is a means of communication; it has been called the "language of business." It provides a special kind of information that is absolutely necessary for performance evaluation, as well as the intelligent management of the limited resources available to any organization.*↩ The accounting process measures resources (labor, materials or rights), and their usage, in terms of a common denominator that is understandable, the dollar.

The purpose of accounting, in more specific terms, is to record, classify, summarize and report the transactions and other financial activities of an organization in a meaningful, structured fashion.

Although usually associated with business, the accounting process provides information for all kinds of organizations for two distinct purposes, one internal, the other external: (1) making management decisions as to the best use of its resources, and (2) reporting to outsiders who have a legitimate interest in the organization's affairs — that is, ***accountability***.

Accountability is the primary component of any financial management structure. All not-for-profits are accountable for the money they receive, accountable to demonstrate (to their benefactors, program beneficiaries, regulatory authorities, "watchdog" organizations or groups, and other financial statement users) that resources are being used effectively to achieve the organization's objectives. They may also be accountable for the use of specific funds restricted by donors for specific purposes (see chapter 13).

The books of account. The core of any accounting and financial reporting system is maintaining accurate and reliable books and records — that is, ***bookkeeping***. There is nothing mysterious or terribly difficult about bookkeeping (although the concept of debits and credits can be tricky, at first). With a little training and guidance from an experienced person, practice and patience, especially with today's easy-to-use software products, almost anyone can learn to do it.

The most basic, bookkeeping system will typically include:

- A cash receipts journal, in which support and revenue are recorded,

- A cash disbursements journal or check register, in which expenses, investments and other expenditures are recorded,

- A general journal, to record noncash and unusual transactions and certain adjustments to the accounts for financial statement preparation purposes, and

- A general ledger, in which all transactions and journal entries are summarized.

Despite the apparent simplicity of a basic, manual bookkeeping system, because of the widespread use of personal computers and availability of a multitude of inexpensive, easy-to-use software packages on the market today (for example, *Peachtree* or *QuickBooks*) that can further simplify the process, improve speed and accuracy and eliminate much of the potential fear and drudgery, almost no one keeps books manually any more, even for the smallest of not-for-profit or business units. Although these products are designed primarily for use by small business units, they are easily adapted, perhaps with professional assistance, for use in small, not-for-profit organizations. Larger, more complex organizations, however, should consider more sophisticated, higher end products specifically designed for not-for-profits, and will likely require professional assistance to select and learn to use the best one for their particular needs.

Financial statement presentation. Authoritative accounting standards applicable to not-for-profit organizations, in general, have undergone a major overhaul during the mid-to-late 1990s. The principal standard now governing the form and content of their general-purpose financial statements (*i.e.*, issued for external users) is Statement No. 117 of the Financial Accounting Standards Board (FASB)* entitled *Financial Statements of Not-for-Profit Organizations*. More detailed guidance as to the general applicability of Statement No. 117 and other applicable FASB standards is contained in the American Institute of Certified Public

---

* The FASB is the independent body established by the accounting profession to keep accounting standard-setting in the United States in the private sector, rather than government.

Accountants' (AICPA) industry audit and accounting guide entitled *Not-for-Profit Organizations* (the AICPA Guide). Specialized guidance as to the accounting practices of not-for-profit colleges, universities and hospitals are in other AICPA industry audit and accounting guides.

The FASB's main objective in Statement No. 117 was to enhance the relevance, understandability, and comparability of financial statements of not-for-profit organizations. Accordingly, it requires that their general-purpose financial statements focus on the entity as a whole and otherwise meet the perceived common needs of external users. To achieve the total entity reporting focus, Statement No. 117, effectively abandoned the previously popular fund accounting approach to financial reporting (although not prohibiting it, *per se)*, and relegated fund accounting to use primarily as a bookkeeping technique and for internal management reporting purposes. (Fund accounting is discussed briefly, later in this chapter.)

FASB Statement No. 117 requires that to conform their general-purpose financial statements with generally accepted accounting principles (GAAP), all not-for-profit organizations need to report their total assets, liabilities, and net assets in a statement of financial position, the change in an organization's net assets in a statement of activities, and the change in its cash and cash equivalents in a statement of cash flows, similarly to for-profit businesses. It also requires that certain organizations defined as "voluntary health and welfare organizations" provide a statement of functional expenses that reports expenses not only by functional classification (as required in the statement of activities of every not-for-profit organization) but also by natural classification.

As one might expect, the term "functional classification" (discussed in detail, below) relates to the function or purpose of the expense, for example, for a specified program or for fundraising, while the term "natural classification" relates to the nature of the expense, for example, salaries, rent, postage and printing. Voluntary health and welfare organizations are those not-for-profit, usually tax exempt, organizations that are formed for the purpose of performing voluntary services primarily to solve societal health and welfare problems or provide other community services, and that derive their revenue primarily not from government or institutional grants but from voluntary contributions from the general public.

Perhaps the most significant features of FASB Statement No. 117 are that it requires (1) that each of three classes of an organization's net assets, *i.e.,* permanently restricted, temporarily restricted, and unrestricted, determined based on the presence and nature, or the absence, of donor-imposed restrictions (see chapter 13), be displayed in the statement of financial position and (2) that the organization's revenues, expenses, gains, and losses, and other changes in *each* of those classes of net assets, be displayed in the statement of activities.

FASB Statement No. 117 allows for considerable flexibility in such things as the titles of the statements of financial position and activities and various other terms and presentation styles. Illustrative general-purpose financial statements are presented in *APPENDIX A* to this **HANDBOOK**.

Summary of specialized accounting principles. Unless clearly excluded by language in an authoritative standard, not-for-profit organizations are generally subject to the accounting, presentation and disclosure requirements applicable to for-profit enterprises. (A detailed summary of general, nonspecialized standards and their applicability or non-applicability to not-for-profit organizations is included in the AICPA Guide.) However, there are a number of specialized accounting principles that apply only to not-for-profit organizations. A summary of the most significant of these follows:

- *Combined financial statements of related entities:* Although local or other subordinate affiliates of larger organizations can and should prepare their own separate financial statements, GAAP contains rules setting forth when central organizations are required or permitted to prepare, or prohibited from preparing, combined or consolidated financial statements, including the accounts of subordinate organizations, as their primary, general-purpose financial statements, depending on the extent of control the central organization is able to exercise over the subordinates. Detailed guidance as to the application of these rules is contained in the AICPA Guide.

- *Contributions, pledges, agency and exchange transactions:* FASB Statement No. 116, *Accounting for Contributions Received and Contributions Made*, defines and governs the accounting for contributions and pledges by both donors and donee organizations. In doing so, it also distinguishes contributions from agency (or custodian) transactions (see chapter 13) and from exchange transactions, both of which are accounted for differently from contributions.

Contributions are recorded and presented and characterized in the statement of activity as either unrestricted or temporarily or permanently restricted, depending upon the donors' stated intentions as to their use. However, subject to certain exceptions (see next paragraph), when the donor specifies more than the intended functional use of the donated funds, but directs the organization to pass them on to a designated beneficiary or beneficiary organization for use, the recipient organization becomes an intermediary or agent. Accordingly, the donated funds are not treated as donations to the recipient organization, but as agency transactions. Agency transactions result in the recognition of a liability to the designated beneficiary and are excluded from contribution revenue in the statement of activities. (When the agency funds are disbursed to the designated beneficiary, the expenditures are likewise excluded from expenses in the statement of activities, and the agency liability is charged, instead.)

There are two exceptions to the foregoing:

1. When funds received and designated as intended for disbursement to a specified entity (or individual) if the donor agrees that the donation is subject to "variance power." "Variance power" refers to an organization's unilateral ability (*i.e.*, without approval of donor, beneficiary or other interested party) to redirect a donor's gift (rather than to return it to the donor) in circumstances when it is judged either impossible or impractical to comply with the donor's wishes, or not consistent with the charitable needs of the community served by the organization.

2. When donors understand and expect that a portion of the donated funds will be withheld by the intermediary entity to cover administrative handling costs, the amount so withheld is classified as contribution revenue.

A third exception remains under deliberation by the FASB at the time of this writing. If adopted as proposed, organizations whose stated purpose is to raise funds for a specified affiliated organization may, under certain conditions, be permitted to report amounts received and remitted to the affiliate, respectively, as contributions revenue and expense.

Exchange transactions include membership dues,* other fees for goods

---

* Since dues are usually collected in advance of providing membership privileges

and services and other contractual arrangements. Federal and other governmental "financial assistance awards" or "grants" are usually (although not universally) treated as exchange transactions. This is based on the view that these so-called "grants" are not gratuitous payments (called "nonreciprocal transfers"), for which no consideration is expected (essentially, the definition of a contribution). Instead, they are viewed, in substance, as contractual arrangements in which the organization agrees to perform a service to achieve the objectives of a government program, usually consistent with the mission of the organization (see chapter 6). Revenue from exchange transactions is recognized on the accrual basis when earned (that is, when the services are rendered), similar to the normal revenue recognition practices of for-profit business enterprises.

Many organizations receive donor's promises (commonly called "pledges") in advance of payment of cash or other assets (see chapter 8). FASB Statement No. 116 provides rules for the recognition in the financial statements of pledges receivable and related contribution revenue. Simply put, pledges are recognizable at their expected net realizable value (discounted for the time value of money, at an appropriate interest rate commensurate with the risk) only when they are (or become) unconditional. A conditional pledge is one to which the donor is effectively uncommitted unless and until a certain stated event occurs or another condition is met. (A pledge is considered unconditional if the likelihood of not meeting a stated condition is remote, for example, if it depends, in substance, merely upon the passage of time.) Amortization (called accretion) of any recorded discount on long-term pledges receivable is recognized in the financial statements as contribution revenue (*not* interest income) as time passes.

According to the AICPA Guide, any reductions in future accounting periods in the expected realizable value of the pledge that are unrelated to discount accretion are written down, and should be reported as bad debts expense (or loss). Any increases in future periods in the expected realizable value of pledges receivable are not recorded except to restore previously recorded valuation writedowns or writeoffs.

---

and services, dues revenue is deferred and amortized over the service period (the dues year). When no significant privileges or services are provided, so-called "dues" are not exchange transactions but are, in substance, contributions and are accounted for accordingly.

Disclosure requirements related to recorded pledges receivable include:

• Amounts due within one year, in one to five years, and in more than five years, and

• The amount of the allowance for uncollectible pledges receivable.

Disclosure requirements related to unrecorded, conditional pledges receivable include:

• The total of amounts promised, and

• A description and amount for each group of promises with similar characteristics (for example, those conditioned on establishing new programs, completing a new building, or raising matching gifts by a specified date).

Bequests are recognized to the extent the value of realizable proceeds is subject to reasonable estimation at the time a court establishes the organization's right to them. Therefore, no accounting recognition is given when an organization has been named in the will of a living person (because the will can always be changed), although it is an unrecorded, conditional pledge and should be disclosed, accordingly, if known (and if material).

Donated property, goods and services (called "in-kind" gifts) are ordinarily recorded as contribution revenue and valued at their fair value at the time of receipt. However, services that do not meet the following criteria are neither valued nor recorded:

• Create or enhance nonfinancial assets, or

• Require specialized skills, are provided by individuals possessing those skills, and would typically need to be purchased if not provided by donation. ("Specialized skills" include those possessed by accountants, architects, carpenters, doctors, electricians, lawyers, nurses, plumbers, teachers, and other professionals and craftsmen.)

Disclosures required regarding contributed services recognized for the period, if material, include:

- A description of the programs or activities for which the donated services were used, their nature and extent, and

- The amount recognized as revenues.

The offsetting charge for recorded revenue for in-kind gifts is to an expense or, if appropriate, to an asset.

Organizations that receive contributions restricted for the acquisition of property and other long-lived assets are also required to adopt and disclose a consistent policy for classification of long-lived assets acquired with such funds (as restricted or unrestricted) in the absence of a donor stipulation in that regard. (Some interpret the donor's restriction to have been met when the asset is purchased, and others interpret the donor's restriction to have been met as the asset is used and depreciated.)

- ***Investments and investment return:*** Not-for-profit organizations are required under FASB Statement No. 124, *Accounting for Certain Investments Held by Not-for-Profit Organizations*, to carry their investments in all debt securities and marketable equity securities (see chapter 9) at fair value with gains and losses from unrealized valuation changes included in the statement of activities.

Among the principal disclosure requirements of Statement No. 124 are:

- The aggregate carrying values of investments by major types (for example, equity securities, U.S. Treasury securities, corporate debt securities, real estate, *etc.*)

- The basis, methods and assumptions used for valuing investments other than marketable equity securities

- The nature of and carrying value of investments that bear a significant concentration of market risk, and

- The separate components of investment return (if material), in at least two categories, including (1) interest and dividends (collectively called "investment income') and (2) net gains or losses, including realized and unrealized.

Statement No. 124 also provides that, in the absence of donor stipulations to the contrary, investment losses on permanently endowed funds (see chapters 6 and 13) be charged to related, temporarily restricted funds, if any, and unrestricted funds, if, not, rather than permitted to invade *corpus*. Any deficiencies so charged also should be disclosed, if material.

The AICPA Guide contains special, rather complex accounting rules for assets, liabilities and related income associated with arrangements under which the not-for-profit organization holds beneficial interests in assets that have been set aside, usually by donors, in trusts. When such beneficial interests in trusteed assets are shared with the donors or other beneficiaries, these arrangements are called "split-interest agreements."

- **Expenses:** FASB Statement No.117 requires that all expenses be charged in the statement of activities to unrestricted funds, and that unrestricted net assets be restored to the extent temporary restrictions have been met (or expired) by showing a transfer of net assets from the temporarily restricted category. A brief description of the nature of the organization's significant programs or program categories, should be disclosed (unless obvious from their title).

As discussed previously in this chapter, Statement 117 also requires that expenses be classified in the statement of activities functionally and, for certain organizations, also presented by natural classification, in a statement of functional expenses. The basis for significant allocations of expenses among functional categories also should be disclosed).

The same rules that apply to the timing of recognition of revenue from contributions and exchange transactions also apply to the recognition of expense for contributions made and other grants and awards. Disbursement of agency funds, however, does not result in recognition of expense because the resultant charge is to the agency liability.

Because they are not contributions, costs incurred in writing and processing applications and contracts for most government and institutional grants and other exchange transactions are classified as administrative, not fundraising, expenses.

- **Restricted net assets:** Statement No. 117 requires disclosure of the amount of net assets temporarily or permanently restricted for each significant program or other purpose.

- **Comparative information for the prior year:** Although not required by GAAP, it is customary for financial statement issuers to present prior year's financial information for comparison to the current year's presentation. However, because comparison of two multi-column presentations can be quite cumbersome, it is common practice to present the prior year's information in a summarized, single-column fashion. When doing so, because it is incomplete, such information should not be characterized as "financial statements" but, instead, should be termed something like "summarized comparative financial information" and accompanied by a disclosure such as:

  > For comparative purposes, certain summarized information for the prior year is presented in the financial statements. However, the prior year's information presented does not include sufficient detail to be in conformity with generally accepted accounting principles. Accordingly, readers who require additional information may should refer to the Organization's previously issued prior year's financial statements from which the summarized information was derived.

Fund accounting. Fund accounting is a rigorous system of accountability for assets whose use is limited either by law or regulation, contract or other obligation, for example, by donors, federal agencies or other grantors, or the organization's own governing board. To keep track of these limitations, and document the organization's compliance therewith, many not-for-profit organizations maintain separate funds on their books of account that are designated for specific purposes. Each fund consists of a self-balancing set of asset, liability, and net asset (fund balance) accounts, including appropriate related revenue, expense and fund transfer accounts, as needed.

↩*It is important to point out that fund accounting represents a bookkeeping technique or control that does not require physical segregation of cash or other assets.* ↪ In fact, as discussed in chapter 7, maintenance of multiple, separate, special-purpose bank accounts, although common, in the absence of a donor-imposed requirement to do so, is to be discouraged in most cases.

As noted earlier in this chapter, before FASB Statement No. 117, not-for-profit organizations usually prepared their general-purpose financial statements for external users on a fund accounting basis. To manage the detail, funds with similar characteristics were typically combined into fund groups. However, funds often contain elements that cross over into more than one of the net asset categories (permanently restricted, temporarily restricted and unrestricted) required by Statement 117. Any given fund could encompass any combination of these three categories of net assets. Accordingly, Statement 117's focus on the three categories of net assets (by restriction) makes presentation of general-purpose financial statements by fund or fund group both awkward and unnecessary, although it is permissible. Fund accounting remains useful — and it is commonly used — but solely for bookkeeping and internal financial reporting (discussed below) to management and the board or its committees.

Examples of some commonly used funds or fund groups include plant (or land, building and equipment) funds, endowment funds (see chapter 13), specified program funds and loan funds (available for lending).

Functional expense classification. GAAP for not-for-profit organizations requires the functional classification of expenses in general-purpose financial statements. Often, however, expenditures do not fit neatly into one functional category or another, and a rational method of allocating expenditures among categories is necessary. The AICPA Guide offers explanations and illustrations of several allocation methods, any one of which may be reasonable or unreasonable in a particular circumstance.

Although other methods of allocation are acceptable, an organization may, for example, allocate expenses functionally based on the following three primary factors (individually or in combination):

1. Time devoted to functional activities may be used to allocate salaries and related expenses based on time records maintained or periodic written estimates by key employees whose time is split among functions; other employees' time may be charged directly to their assigned function(s) based on management's estimates,

2. Space occupied by employees or designated for certain functions may be used, possibly in combination with the time factor, to allocate rent, utilities and other occupancy costs, telephone and similar expenses, and

3. Charges for such items as meetings, travel, printing, postage and other identifiable "project" costs may be allocated, when appropriate, among two or more functions based on management's reasonable estimates. These allocations should be supported by appropriate documentation of the basis for the allocation (see discussion, below, about the AICPA's Statement of Position 98-2).

Direct charges ordinarily should be made to the proper account classifications when an expense is first recorded on the books. It is recommended that time and space allocations be made and revised on a year-to-date basis each time financial statements are prepared.

Some organizations put all salaries and overhead in the functional administrative (commonly called "management and general") category for the sake of simplicity. However, if these amounts are substantial, such shortcuts are not recommended because the results will be misleading and may cause unduly adverse evaluations of the organization's performance.

Public charities must compete for precious few donor dollars. Those who evaluate the performance of these organizations look for something economists call "target efficiency," that is, concentrating expenditures in program categories consistent with the organization's mission. Conversely, they are critical of excessive expenditures in the support categories of fundraising and administration. They do not like to think that donors' money is lining the pockets of professional fundraisers or executives (like William Aramony). Likewise, they do not like waste. Therefore, the functional classification of expenses into program and support services (or activities) categories is of substantial concern to sophisticated donors and prospective donors, as well as other financial statement users, such as "watchdog" groups and regulators, who watch out for their interests.

The National Charities Information Bureau (NCIB) functions as a source of information for donors about national public charities (see chapters 4 and 14) — a public "watchdog" organization — much like the Better Business Bureau functions in the business world. It cautions charities and donors to be wary of unsupportable allocations of fundraising costs to educational program categories, an area where the NCIB has perceived abuses. State regulators, likewise, have been extremely interested in perceived abuses in this area and remain so, today (see chapter 12), and some states have bodies similar to NCIB in place to evaluate organizations for target efficiency for the benefit of prospective donors.

As a result of pressure from NCIB and other "watchdog" organizations and regulators, the AICPA recognized the possibility of abuse by misallocating fundraising costs to program categories and issued highly restrictive and complex standards in its Statement of Position (SOP) 98-2, entitled *Accounting for Costs of Activities of Not-for-Profit Organizations and State and Local Governmental Entities That Include Fund Raising.*

Briefly, SOP 98-2 requires that costs incurred in connection with fundraising activities may be allocated or charged directly to those other functional categories deemed to have benefited therefrom only if certain criteria are met as to purpose, audience, and content (including a call to action that furthers the program objectives). These fundraising activities may include, for example, direct mail, telephone solicitation, door-to-door canvassing, telethons, and special events. (See chapter 6.) If any of the criteria are not met, *all costs of the activity are reported as fundraising*, including costs that otherwise might be considered program or administrative costs (except that costs of goods or services provided (for example, a meal served at a special fundraising event), are not reported as fundraising. It also requires certain disclosures about allocations of "joint" costs involving fundraising, usually to an education related program category.

Allocation methods used by organizations that incur "joint" costs associated with fundraising activities a portion of which it would like to allocate to other functional categories, generally, should follow these guidelines or similarly logical and supportable alternatives. However, for smaller organizations that do not allocate joint costs associated with fundraising (therefore, not subject to SOP 98-2), simplification of the procedures is encouraged — when no material distortion is likely to result, and the overall objective will be met. For example, employees may make periodic estimates (which should be documented in writing) as to the percentage of their time spent in each functional activity, rather than record time daily on timesheets.

Because it is extremely technical and limited in its applicability, however, coverage of the provisions of SOP 98-2 in any detail is beyond the scope of this **HANDBOOK**. It is reproduced in its entirety as an appendix to the AICPA Guide. However, preparers of financial statements of not-for-profit organizations that engage in certain types of fundraising activities that include components associated with program or administrative activities or services need to be familiar with it.

Internal financial reporting. So far, the focus of this chapter has been on general-purpose, external financial reporting. GAAP standards were developed to serve the needs of external financial statement users. The presentation and disclosure requirements of these standards do not apply, however, to internal financial reporting.

↤ *The needs and objectives of management and the board for financial information to enable them to perform their management and oversight functions effectively are quite different from those of external financial statement users.* ↦ They are also quite different among different organizations and for the same organization at different stages of its development. Therefore, as flexible as is the presentation model for external reporting under FASB Statement No. 117, there is considerably more diversity of presentation styles that may be suitable for internal reporting purposes.

Although there are no authoritative standards that apply to internal financial reporting, for the reports to be used effectively for management or oversight purposes, some recommended principles to observe are as follows:

- Interim (for example, monthly or quarterly) financial reports should be prepared and distributed timely to those in the organization who are responsible for management and financial oversight.

- The frequency of interim reporting periods should be based on balancing needs with practical considerations. (For example, quarterly reports would be appropriate for smaller organizations and for more financially strong, stable organizations with more well planned and dependable fundraising campaigns and predictable operating results, or when the financial reporting process is complicated. On the other hand, internal monthly reports would be more appropriate when financial stability is weak, despite substantial resources or high transactional volume, when fundraising is erratic and operations more volatile, or when the reporting process is simple.)

- If practical, internal financial statements should be prepared on the same accrual basis of accounting (unless necessary accrual adjustments are not ordinarily material), in accordance with the same GAAP accounting measurement policies as used to prepare the annual, general-purpose financial statements intended for external distribution.

- Although the traditional disclosures required by GAAP for external, general purpose reporting are ordinarily omitted in internal financial reports, more detailed quantitative information is ordinarily presented. However, the quantitative detail presented should be summarized into totals or subtotals that can be matched readily to the more aggregated amounts presented in the external financial statements.

- The most significant feature of the internal financial statements should be the presentation of budget information, budget variances and explanations of the variances, together with descriptions of corrective actions taken or planned with respect thereto (see chapter 4).

- Budget variance analysis ordinarily should be focused primarily on the year-to-date amounts, rather than the most recent interim period (*i.e.*, the latest month or quarter).

- Internal financial reports ordinarily should be accompanied by a memorandum containing interpretive analysis of the treasurer or other responsible preparer explaining the significance of the reported results and their implications for the future.

CHAPTER 4: BUDGETING

Building a good structure, no matter how solid the foundation, cannot proceed without a plan. A budget is a plan of action, a blueprint for the coming year, expressed in dollars. *Other than the integrity of volunteer management (and staff, if any), the budget should be the most fundamental and pervasive element in your organization's internal control.*

Sadly, in many not-for-profit organizations, the budgeting process is viewed as a tedious and meaningless requirement that is given little or no attention by anyone in management other than the treasurer. Board approval is by "rubber stamp," so to speak. Such budgets often reflect no more thought than merely rounding last year's operating results. Following adoption, they are generally filed away and not looked at again. *This type of budgeting serves no useful purpose!*

Elements of a budget. *To be effective, as it should be, a budget must be taken seriously and be a joint effort and commitment by many people.* It must be a working document that forms the basis for action. It must consider known facts and circumstances in the context of realistic, attainable goals and objectives identified by management for the organization.

Properly used, a budget minimizes waste and inefficiency and provides direction. Many people think of a budget primarily as a means of controlling expenses, and use it to establish accountability and control — to monitor performance.

But to get the full benefit of the planning features of the budgeting process, it must be more than just a control over the outflow and a mere expression of goals. No less significantly, it should also be used to plan and control inflows — revenues, that is. (Planning effective fundraising campaigns is discussed briefly in chapter 6.) When used effectively, a budget affords a benchmark to alert management to any indications that its fundraising and other financial goals may not be met, and it allows it to measure progress, anticipate problems and formulate timely corrective action.

In summary, for a budget to function well in these various ways, four elements must be present:

1. The budget should be thoughtfully conceived, supported by those who will carry it out, and intelligently reviewed and approved by both the finance committee and the board.

2. The budget should be prepared in at least the same level of detail as, and broken down into periods that correspond with, periodic interim financial statements.

3. Periodic financial statements must be prepared timely, with budget *vs.* actual comparisons and variances shown; significant variances must be explained.

4. The board or finance committee must be prepared to take remedial action whenever warranted.*

It is more important, particularly for larger organizations, to budget expenses functionally, rather than by natural category (see chapter 3), although, if practical, it is best to do it both ways.

The NCIB is the nation's leading "watchdog" organization. Its mission is to promote informed giving and charitable integrity to enable more contributors to make sound giving decisions. The NCIB has issued its "Standards in Philanthropy" against which it evaluates the accountability and financial reporting policies and practices of selected charities, and it reports its findings to inquirers, principally prospective donors. Preparation of a proper annual budget, approved by the board, is the subject of NCIB's Standard in Philanthropy No. 9.

When setting out to prepare a budget, it is best to involve several people who will participate in the next year's operations, and ask each other questions like:

•   What would we like to accomplish this year?

•   How will we do it?

•   How much will it cost to do it?

•   How much support (contributions) or other revenue will it produce?

---

*   When budgeted expenditures are exceeded, but no corrective adjustment in future periods is contemplated, it is preferable to treat the excess as an approved variance, rather than to increase the budget.

The answers to these questions become what is often referred to as a "zero-based" budget (which is the best kind). This means the budget was built from the ground up, rather than by starting with last year's numbers and making adjustments.

Unless you expect your organization to do exactly the same as it did last year (most unlikely in today's rapidly changing society) last year's operating results (or worse, last year's budget) is a bad place to start the budgeting process. *➥In fact, if last year's results are known, you are starting the budgeting too late. The budget's utility as a control device is severely diminished if it is not in place for the entire period it covers.*➥

It is common for not-for-profits to budget for breakeven operations— income equal to expenses. In doing so, there are no "rainy day" provisions. The importance of being conservative — and mindful of local economic trends — in estimating contribution revenues when budgeting this way cannot be overemphasized. A revenue shortfall can be financially disastrous. Since contributions are often heavily concentrated in the latter part of the year (because of donors seeking last minute income tax deductions), it is usually too late to adjust spending when such a revenue shortfall is finally realized.

On the other hand, when you are conservative, contributions often exceed budgeted expenditures, and the result is the building of healthy reserves that may cushion future unexpected costs or revenue deficiencies, or be used for special projects. *➥It is far wiser, therefore, to plan and budget for better than break-even performance —that's right, profits —to enable the organization to continue its important work in the event of a subsequent lean year.*➥

Budget benchmarks. When budgeting, consider the following excerpts from NCIB's Standard in Philanthropy No. 6 (including selected NCIB interpretive language in *italics*):

> The organization's use of funds should reflect consideration of current and future needs and resources in planning for program continuity. The organization should:
>
> a. spend at least 60% of annual expenses for program activities;*

---

* Some states require more than 60%, and 75% is generally considered ideal.

b. insure that fund-raising expenses, in relation to fund-raising results, are reasonable over time;

   ...Overall, an organization's fund-raising expense should be reasonable in relation to the contributions received, which could include indirect contributions...

c. have net assets available for use in the following fiscal year not usually more than twice the current year's expenses or twice the next year's budget, whichever is higher;

   *...Organizations may accumulate funds in the interest of prudent management. Accumulation of such funds in excess of the Standard may be justified in special circumstances.**

Accordingly, many established, financially strong organizations maintain up to two years' estimated operating expenses in reserve. However, a delicate balancing act occurs when soliciting large donations. If the organization's balance sheet looks too weak, people are leery about giving it money; if the balance sheet looks too strong, they think it doesn't need it, that it is accumulating wealth instead of performing the services for which it exists. To strike the right balance, therefore, this author recommends that organizations dependent on fundraising seek to maintain in reserve — as a goal — approximately one year's operating budget.

Capital budgeting. It may be necessary to budget for cash outflows that are outside normal operating activities and that are not accounted for as expenses or charged against the operating budget. Organizations that expend substantial amounts for land and buildings, equipment, libraries or other long-lived assets (called "capital assets" or "capital expenditures" — and often comprising major, distinct capital projects) should plan for such expenditures, and their funding, through capital budgeting.

Organizations that prepare their operating budgets (as they should) on an accrual basis ordinarily will include a provision for depreciation. Since the depreciation charge will not represent an expenditure of current revenues, it can be viewed as a replacement reserve for wasting capital assets — or

---

* Net assets that are permanently restricted or restricted for use in future periods beyond the next year, including long-term pledges receivable, and those invested in property or other long-lived assets, are generally understood to be excluded from this standard.

a part of a capital budget. This is why some people suggest that depreciation can be a source of funds.

Although annual capital budgets are recommended when appropriate, capital projects often span periods greater than a single fiscal year, making long-range planning necessary.

Strategic planning. Even without long-range capital projects, your most significant organizational goals ordinarily go far beyond one year. Therefore, it is ordinarily healthy to extend the budget planning process, including both operating and capital budgets beyond the immediately succeeding year, say, to five years. Although the process may be less formal for smaller organizations, a broader-based, long-range strategic planning process is recommended for those with more substantial financial goals and resources. ↦ *Unlike the annual budget, which, once approved, is best left unchanged for the entire year, a long-range financial plan should be far more flexible and dynamic; it should be updated and revised at least annually as circumstances change.* ↤

Financial goals are best achieved by planning and budgeting. In fact, the value of planning in managing any kind of organization is well documented and virtually unarguable; it can help a great deal in keeping your organization focused on its mission. Long-range strategic planning is like chicken soup — *it couldn't hurt!*

CHAPTER 5: CONTROLLING CASH RECEIPTS

One area commonly of concern in public charities — because of certain risks discussed below — is contributions and other cash receipts (in this context, "cash" is a term generally understood to include coin, currency and checks). Accordingly, as its title suggests, this chapter concentrates primarily on controlling against the risk of unrecorded cash contributions and other revenues and receipts.

⇥ *One can easily see that the principal control objective regarding cash receipts, broadly stated, is to reasonably assure that they be properly recorded and deposited in a bank account of the organization.* ↤

To identify risk, one merely asks, "What can go wrong (that could have a significant or material effect)?" Possible answers: cash receipts might be lost or misappropriated and therefore, unrecorded; they might also be recorded in an incorrect amount and/or misclassified.

Risks and control objectives are qualitatively the same for donations received in currency, coin or checks. Therefore, it is best if, as soon as possible, checks received by the organization are logged in and stamped with the organization's restrictive endorsement, "*For Deposit Only*," and then deposited the same day. Checks payable to the organization should always be deposited and **never** be endorsed over to an individual or another entity. If possible, as in larger organizations, the deposits should be made by a different individual from the one who opens the mail and logs in the daily receipts.

But the risks of loss or misappropriation are inherently greater with currency than checks; it's a matter of degree. Those risks are most effectively mitigated, however, by establishing policies and procedures that have the following characteristics:

- They should require adequate accountability from those collecting or otherwise handling the currency and checks, and

- They should limit the dollar amount of currency that may be held — and the length of time it can be held — by any one individual until control can be more securely established by depositing the currency and checks received in the organization's bank account.

For example, special fundraising events frequently entail the sale of tickets to such activities as dinners, dances, theater parties, races or ballgames. Payment is often made in currency, particularly for small amounts. For these activities, physical safeguards (or security) and accountability control should be established over the tickets and proceeds as early as possible. That means unissued tickets should be kept locked and, immediately upon issuance for sale or further distribution, the custodian should record the name of, and the number of tickets issued to, each solicitor or other recipient.

The custodian should obtain the signature of each solicitor acknowledging receipt and responsibility to account for all tickets, sold and unsold, and to turn in all proceeds, in accordance with periodic, established deadlines. Reporting forms should be provided. If the tickets are sequentially pre-numbered (which is preferable), the ticket numbers should likewise be recorded upon issuance and subsequently accounted for. The number of tickets issued to any one individual between accountings should be limited. All proceeds turned in, including coin, currency and checks, should be deposited in the organization's bank account absolutely as soon as practical.

Many people who give cash donations can be expected to request a receipt for income tax purposes. It is therefore recommended that the organization provide each ticket seller or solicitor with books of duplicate receipts (the retained copy being the initial record of each contribution) to issue to donors on its behalf. Control is maximized if the receipts are preprinted with the organization's name and/or logo and pre-numbered so there can be a record made of receipts assigned and a periodic accountability for them, as well.

Similar controls are applied in connection with leaving receptacles in strategic locations for donors to deposit coins and small bills. In this type of fundraising program, proceeds are all coin or currency, no checks. Because the receptacles are left in the hands of others (for example, local retailers) to be filled, it is important that their names, addresses and telephone numbers be recorded at the time of distribution, together with the number of receptacles left. This will not necessarily prevent pilferage of the receptacles, or their contents, but will serve to establish responsibility and accountability therefor. The receptacles should be designed such that they are difficult to "counterfeit" or to open without leaving evidence of unauthorized entry.

↜ *The key to controlling all cash receipts is establishing a record at the earliest practical moment, for contributions, preferably the point of donation, limiting the amount of cash held by any single individual —and getting the money into the bank as soon as possible.* ↢ Another important rule should be to deposit all cash receipts intact and never to permit disbursements to be made from them. Such practice bypasses controls over both receipts and disbursements and increases the risk of unrecorded transactions. Except for petty cash, all disbursements should be made by check (see chapter 7).

"Lockbox" services. An extremely effective way to overcome certain risks and difficulties commonly experienced by organizations that engage in fundraising campaigns that produce high volumes of small checks in the mail is to use a bank "lockbox" service to receive and process the mail responses to fundraising campaigns. Otherwise, these checks take a long time to process, record and deposit, especially for organizations with limited staff or only volunteer staff. During this time, these mail receipts are highly susceptible to loss or theft — and the dollars that they represent cannot earn interest or be spent on program services, or used merely to "pay the bills," until they are deposited.

A bank "lockbox" service involves donors mailing their contributions (usually in pre-addressed envelopes provided by the charity) to the organization, not at its regular office address, but at an assigned mailbox number at the bank. Bank employees process the checks received (under the highly controlled conditions one would expect at a bank), deposit them in the organization's bank account quickly — usually within 24 hours of receipt — and prepare and send reports to the organization, so it can begin earning interest on — or spending — the money as soon as possible.

Some organizations tend to avoid using "lockbox" services because of the appearance of high costs in the form of transaction-based bank charges. (Even with today's technology, it is still a labor-intensive process, although likely to become less so). ↢ *Nevertheless, when one considers the risk of loss or misappropriation, or the costs (although often immeasurable) of (1) the temporary loss of use of the money and (2) the deployment of limited staff or even volunteers (either of whom could be raising money or providing program services, instead, or who could be getting burned out from the tedium of processing all those checks), a "lockbox" service is probably well worth its cost.* ↢ And, as discussed in chapter 9, the bank charges may be negotiable.

41

CHAPTER 6: FUNDRAISING

Fundraising is a specialized form of marketing. Since this **HANDBOOK** is not about marketing, *per se*, it discusses only selected highlights regarding fundraising because of its significant effect on budgeting and its other financial implications and consequences.

↪*Organizations often become quite effective at using the budget process to manage their expenses, but many are relatively inept at managing their revenues. Managing revenues is a necessary element of sound financial planning in for-profit and not-for-profit entities alike.*↩ Since fundraising (often called "development") is the marketing function of not-for-profit organizations, successful fundraising employs marketing concepts and techniques. In larger organizations, a person with specialized marketing training usually leads the function. One of the most universally accepted marketing techniques, which is utilized by development executives, involves maintaining donor databases with significant data about the organization's donors and their giving patterns and motivators, and segmenting the data into meaningful categories to target them differently. These databases become significant resources for the organization and must be protected against loss, damage or unauthorized use (see chapter 15).

Professional fundraisers. Many organizations, particularly smaller ones that are short on resources, contract for the services of outside professional fundraisers. Use of outside professional fundraisers can be fraught with dangers and, therefore, should be approached with extreme caution. Just as in many other areas of business — and life — there are those who are honorable and reliable, and there are those who engage in unethical practices, are dishonest, exploitive, and often predatory. National and local news reports are full of stories warning potential donors about unscrupulous fundraisers, often representing fake charities.

↪*Almost nothing can do more damage to your organization's image and reputation in the community than an unscrupulous, so-called "professional" fundraiser.*↩

Many outside fundraisers (telemarketers, for example) require that they be compensated in the form of a percentage commission based the amount of funds they raise, often exorbitantly, taking 50% or more of the proceeds. The National Society of Fund Raising Executives (NSFRE), as the name implies, is a national professional association of fundraisers. *According to NSFRE, it is **unethical** for a fundraising professional to accept compensation based on the amount of funds raised.* The NSFRE's "Statements of Ethical Principles" and its "Standards of Professional Practice Principles" (as last amended, November 1997) provide that it members:

- "...put charitable mission above personal gain, accepting compensation by salary or set fee only"

- "...work for a salary or fee, not percentage-based compensation or a commission"

- "...may accept performance-based compensation, such as bonuses, provided that such bonuses are...*not based on a percentage of philanthropic funds raised*" [emphasis added]

- "...shall not pay, seek or accept finder's fees, commissions or percentage-based compensation for obtaining philanthropic funds and shall, to the best of their ability, discourage...such payments."

To compound matters, many so-called "professional" fundraising businesses attempt to justify their exorbitant commission rates based on the additional so-called "administrative services" they provide in the form of actually collecting the proceeds, paying themselves, including certain "allowable" expense reimbursements, and remitting the net proceeds, often with no or inadequate accountability to the beneficiary organization. Thus the beneficiary organization never knows if it is receiving what it is due under its agreement with the fundraiser.

What's more, accounting standards require presenting the contributions raised and fundraiser commissions in the financial statements gross, not net. Consequently, if a substantial portion of the organization's support were raised in this fashion (for example, subject to a 50% fundraiser's commission) and properly reported, the ratio of fundraising expense to total expenses undoubtedly would exceed industry standards or other financial statement user expectations. These expectations ordinarily limit fund-raising to approximately 15% of total expenses. Exceeding this "rule–of–thumb" would likely invite criticism from donors, regulators and "watchdog" organizations that might impair your organization's ability to raise funds more legitimately in the future.

44

Fundraising from the general public — particularly with outside professional fundraisers — is heavily regulated at the state, and sometimes local, level. In fact, even public appeals for volunteer services are often subject to state or local regulation (see chapter 12). State regulations often impose requirements or restrictions on disclosures to be made by professional fundraisers, sometimes including requiring them to disclose to prospects that they are being paid for their services. State regulators can be very touchy about violations — and the organizations are often held responsible and bear the consequences.

↦ *Therefore, organizations intending to engage professional fundraisers (or fundraising "consultants") should ascertain, in advance, whether the proposed fundraiser (or "consultant") is duly registered in the organization's home state and any other states in which it intends to solicit funds on the organization's behalf, and they should obtain appropriate written representations in that regard and that the proposed fundraiser (or "consultant") will observe all disclosure requirements and restrictions, as provided by law.* ↤

Planned giving. In a planned giving fundraising campaign, the organization works to obtain large, long-term commitments from prospective donors to support future activities of the organization. These may include having the organization named as a beneficiary of a life insurance policy, or in a will, or of one of a number of types of special trusts created by the donor. Many of these arrangements appeal to prospective donors based on expected income tax or estate planning benefits. It is ordinarily necessary that those soliciting these kinds of gifts be knowledgeable about such instruments and their legal and tax implications, or that they be assisted by knowledgeable professionals.
It is likewise important, as a means of avoiding risk of liability, and to assure the confidence of the donor, to recommend strongly that donors seek counsel with their own legal and tax advisors before agreeing to such commitments.

Soliciting endowment gifts. Sometimes planned giving arrangements involve endowments. Endowment gifts are ordinarily of substantial size and, therefore, generally require substantial effort to obtain. Before embarking on a campaign to solicit endowment gifts — and expending the volunteer time and other resources to do so — the treasurer should advise the board, and others in the organization who are responsible for fundraising recommendations or decisions, to consider seriously whether endowment gifts are consistent with the organization's needs.

Endowments are most beneficial when obtained to provide for long-term financial requirements (for example, to replace a building in 20 years) because this enables the expendable income part of the fund to compound over time and grow exponentially. (Short-term financial requirements, on the other hand, are funded most efficiently by obtaining current donations that are immediately expendable.) When endowments are used to fund short-term needs, the income is siphoned off and spent too quickly, before any meaningful compounding takes place. In addition, because the funds need to be spent sooner, there is no time for a reasonable level risk tolerance that is necessary to take advantage of normal mid-range to long range investment market cycles (see chapter 9). Accordingly, the need to invest only in highly liquid, low risk instruments further impairs the potential for earning (and spending) investment return. The effect of all this is tying up the endowment *corpus* (usually a lot of money) for a long, long time, for very little return — a highly inefficient use, therefore, of the *corpus*. As a result, it is also a highly inefficient use of the resources expended to raise the endowment funds.

Small contributions. When soliciting small donations, care should be taken not to invite donor restrictions (see chapter 13) unnecessarily. Assuring compliance with them tends to become an accounting nightmare, particularly for smaller or understaffed organizations. Alternatively, it is best to appeal to prospective donors by merely telling them the kinds of program expenditures that might be made with their donated funds, but not asking them to select their preferences from a menu. If they feel strongly enough to restrict the use of their donations, they will surely tell you, and the organization can comply.

Federated campaigns. Among other sources of funds are the local United Way and other federated campaigns, for example, the Combined Federal Campaign. These organizations typically sponsor "in-the-workplace" fundraising campaigns the results of which are allocated and distributed among qualifying charities that participate. To qualify to participate (*i.e.*, receive allocations of funds), there are usually objective financial and other criteria that must be demonstrably met, for example, an annual audit.

A less burdensome way of participating in a federated campaign is to communicate directly among your organization's constituency, asking them to designate that their donations to the federated campaign be directed to your organization. (This is ordinarily done after deducting a service charge of, say, 10%.) This technique is effective in combating the potential effect of on-the-job pressures to give to the federated campaign resulting in dividing the available donation budgets of individuals. By directing their contributions to your organization, donors get a double "bang for their buck."

Government grants. Many organizations seek to obtain funds necessary to achieve their goals by applying for government (or institutional) grants. The effective writing of grant requests requires special knowledge and skill and, therefore, ordinarily should be performed by someone with the appropriate training and experience. Often, outside consultants are engaged for this purpose, and the normal diligence should be exercised to check out the consultant's credentials. While consultants' fees and other costs incurred for writing grant applications are technically not "fundraising" for financial reporting purposes, it is equally inappropriate to compensate such consultants (or employees) as a percentage of grant proceeds.

In addition, government grants, generally come with a number of statutory, regulatory or contractual compliance "strings" attached (see chapter 12) — especially when federal money is involved. For example, by statute (the "Single Audit Act of 1984," as amended), aggregate annual expenditures of federal financial assistance awards in excess of $300,000 expose the organization to additional auditing and reporting requirements. Failure to comply with these requirements, among other possible penalties, may result in a liability to return grant funds, even after they have been dispensed in good faith. This requires that someone in the organization be familiar with all applicable grant compliance requirements and monitor compliance. Accordingly, grant compliance is often quite costly. Frequently, inexperienced or otherwise unskilled individuals fail to include sufficient funds in the grant request to cover the costs of administering the grant, like additional audit costs — costs that are ordinarily reimbursable — resulting in negative cash flow to the organization.

Also, the board is responsible to exercise sufficient care to assure itself that grants applied for are for purposes that are consistent with the needs and mission of the organization. *↦ Too often, to increase his or her perceived value to the organization and compensation (even when not directly linked by agreement), an ambitious (to choose a kind word) executive director applies for a government grant merely to be able to demonstrate to the board how much money was raised. Frequently, the funds raised in such circumstances not only have nothing to do with the organization's mission, but because the grant request was hastily or otherwise inartfully prepared, the costs of administering the grant exceed its proceeds. ↤*

CHAPTER 7: CONTROLLING CASH DISBURSEMENTS

In this chapter, we discuss other controls against loss or misappropriation of cash — using the term "cash" in a narrower sense than before, primarily relating to funds on deposit in banks. The term, as used in this (and the following) chapter, however, also should be understood to include "cash equivalents," which includes money market accounts on deposit with brokerage firms, and certain short-term and highly liquid investments, such as certificates of deposit, that mature in three months or less.

In deciding what controls are needed, once again, we ask ourselves, "What could go wrong?" The main risks usually faced in this area are that checks might be issued:

- By individuals not authorized to do so

- In payment of goods or services from which the organization did not or will not benefit

- Not in accordance with the organization's purpose, or

- Not provided for in the budget.

Also, checks (whether properly authorized or not) might be either unrecorded, recorded in improper amounts or misclassified on the books.

↦*Consequently, the basic control objectives relative to cash disbursements are to obtain reasonable assurance that they are made only in accordance with management's authorization and the organization's purpose and goals, in amounts that properly represent organization obligations, and that they are properly recorded.* ↤

Proper use of the budget is one of the most effective ways of controlling many of these risks. Because of the budget's significance in this and other respects, all of chapter 4 is devoted to it. Other practical suggestions for managing these risks are contained in the next several paragraphs.

Special-purpose bank accounts. With some exceptions (discussed below), as explained in chapter 3, it is generally not advisable to maintain several special-purpose bank accounts, and to use only one active checking account, so as not to unduly complicate the monthly bank reconciliation process and make errors and improprieties more difficult to uncover. Alternatively, it is best to adopt bookkeeping controls to keep track of funds designated for special purposes (*i.e.* fund accounting).

Signature authority. It is recommended that check-signing authority be restricted to those few individuals for whom it is necessary, bearing in mind that you may need one or two alternate signers in case of temporary inaccessibility of a primary signer. Ordinarily, the primary check signer should be the treasurer. If possible, it is best if the person who keeps the books (if not the treasurer) does not have signature authority.

↦ *A policy requiring dual signatures on all checks can be an effective control against unauthorized disbursements and is recommended but only when applied for **all** checks drawn from a particular account and in the presence of two closely related safeguards.* ↤ These safeguards are:

1. The common practice (often justified based on the "difficulty" of getting two signatures) of allowing one signer to pre-sign blank checks must be strictly prohibited. (This practice *totally disables* dual signatures as a control procedure. But with only a minimal amount of advance planning, the so-called difficulty is easily overcome.)

2. Check signers must independently take responsibility for reviewing all supporting documentation and satisfy themselves that the disbursement is proper. (All documentation should then be canceled when paid and retained to prevent duplicate payments.)

The control effectiveness of requiring dual signatures is severely diminished when it is applied only for checks over a certain size, and when the related account balance often substantially exceeds the single signature limit. This practice is ineffective as a control in these circumstances because of the ease with which a single signer may overcome it with limited authority merely by issuing more than one check, the aggregate value of which exceeds the limit. When it is a practical necessity to make limited funds available on a single signature basis, a better control alternative would be to maintain a separate account at a fixed balance, as small as possible in the circumstances (seasonally adjusted, if necessary), and replenished as often as needed. The person with limited authority would not be able to disburse funds from larger accounts without a second signature. (Such fixed balance funds are called "imprest" funds.) Of course, this arrangement would be an acceptable exception to the general rule-of-thumb against special-purpose bank accounts.

The problem of obtaining second signatures timely, when necessary, is mitigated by better planning and communication, and by more aggresively seeking more typical business credit terms from vendors.

Physical safeguards. ↦*Because of technological developments in word processing and "desk-top publishing" software, anyone who has a computer and an inexpensive printer can make excellent bogus checks for fraudulent disbursements.*↤ Couple this with the fact that the sheer volume of checks processed through the necessarily automated systems of the nation's banks and clearing houses makes the inspection of checks for authorized signatures to any significant degree a virtual impossibility. Banks have, in fact, denied liability for losses from paying forged checks when it could be shown that the depositor had not taken ordinarily prudent steps to protect against such losses, for example, by safeguarding supplies of unissued checks under lock and key.

Effective protection against unauthorized use of blank checks is also obtained through numerical accountability. To achieve numerical accountability, it is necessary to maintain a policy requiring that checks be issued only in numerical sequence and that checking the integrity of the sequence be part of the bank reconciliation review process (discussed below).

As also discussed in regard to a dual signature policy, any control ordinarily to be expected from numerical accountability is rendered virtually ineffective by either of the following ill-advised practices, adopted for the sake of convenience:

• Giving out blocks of blank checks to different officers for issuance on an "as needed" basis, or

• Issuing post-dated checks to vendors.

And these practices make the bank reconciliation process unnecessarily more complicated. ↦*Therefore, to maintain proper control over cash disbursements, to the extent possible, it is best that all checks from a particular bank account be issued by, the same person from the same central location.* ↵

↳ *However, when every employee in every vendor company that processes checks issued by the organization, and everyone in the organization who handles deposit slips or the bank statement (whether they have access to canceled or unused checks or not) has access to the organization's bank account number, normal (or even elaborate) controls relative to safeguarding supplies of unused checks, segregation of duties and required approvals, do not afford sufficiently effective protection against counterfeiting checks, —and this says nothing of those in the banking system who may be inclined to be dishonest! That is why the* **bank reconciliation process is so critically important.** ↵

Bank reconciliations. The monthly bank reconciliation process, when properly done, can be the most effective control over many of the risks associated with cash disbursements, as well as receipts.

↳ *Unless the organization is able to keep its bank balances (and, therefore, its exposure to losses) near zero (without any overdraft access to a line of credit), the bank reconciliation process is the only effective way to detect unauthorized disbursements, if they occur.* ↵ However, because segregation of duties and other typical controls do not effectively prevent check counterfeiting, especially by someone in a position to conceal it (by recording checks improperly), the bank reconciliation process will likewise be ineffective unless it is done — and independently reviewed — both properly and timely.

↳ *It cannot be overemphasized that if bank reconciliations are not performed timely and properly, reconciling items that might represent unrecorded and unauthorized cash disbursements will not be investigated timely and thoroughly, and the organization will be seriously exposed to loss.* ↵

Bank reconciliations should be done as soon as practical following receipt of the bank statement. If it is impractical to have them performed by someone other than the bookkeeper, they should be critically reviewed, timely each month, by the treasurer or other responsible individual not involved with the daily bookkeeping.

A critical review of the bank reconciliation ordinarily should include comparing payee names on cancelled checks to those entered on the books, inspecting endorsements, and test tracing entries from the books to supporting documentation to obtain reasonable assurance that the funds were received by the intended recipients. Checks outstanding (or deposits "in transit") for unusually long periods, or other questionable reconciling items, should be investigated timely, and appropriate entries made or other actions taken.

Petty cash funds. Petty cash funds are usually used to make small currency and coin expenditures when it is impractical or impossible to use checks. Petty cash expenditures and funds should always be limited to the minimal extent necessary and practical to meet short-term needs, and these funds always should be maintained on an imprest basis. For all disbursements from the fund, receipts should be obtained, or vouchers prepared, and kept together with the fund until replenishment, such that the total of cash and vouchers equals the fixed (imprest) fund balance at all times. Only one individual (preferably not the bookkeeper, if possible) should control and access the fund as custodian, and it should be kept locked.

Replenishment (often called "reimbursement") of petty cash funds should be made by check payable to something like "Petty Cash," "Petty Cash Custodian" or "John Doe, Petty Cashier," never just to "John Doe." As soon as practical following replenishment, all vouchers should be canceled and retained just like the documentation supporting other checks.

Once again, the general rule about multiple, special-purpose bank accounts notwithstanding, for practical purposes, sometimes it may be desirable to maintain a special, imprest checking account to permit smaller, routine expenditures of a "petty cash" nature that, because of lower risk of misappropriation, are subject to less stringent controls than the "normal" disbursements. For example, a separate checking account may be set up that permits disbursements of no more than, say, $100, with more readily accessible authorized signers who are not authorized to sign larger checks. Like the petty cash fund, control is maintained by limiting the balance in the account and by requiring higher level approvals for replenishment checks.

CHAPTER 8: PLEDGES RECEIVABLE

This chapter deals with maintaining appropriate records of, and other procedures relative to, pledges receivable that will optimize the organization's assurance that they will be collected timely. It also supplements the discussion in chapter 3 of the rules and conditions for recording pledges and including them as assets and revenues in the financial statements of the organization.

To permit accounting recognition of a promise as contribution revenue, and a related pledge receivable, the organization must have documentary evidence that it was made unconditionally. According to the AICPA Guide:

> Such evidence may be included in written or verifiable oral communications, including (a) written agreements, (b) pledge cards, and (c) oral promises documented by tape recordings, written contemporaneous registers, follow-up written confirmations, and other means that permit subsequent verification of the oral communications. A communication that does not indicate clearly whether it is a promise is considered an unconditional promise to give if it indicates an unconditional intention to give that is legally enforceable. Promises to give that do not discuss the specific time or place for the contribution but that are otherwise clearly unconditional in nature should be considered unconditional promises to give.

Of course, for substantial pledges, written communications are strongly recommended, including all conditions, restrictions and other terms, not the least significant of which is an understanding as to when they are expected to be paid.

A communication informing the organization that a bequest to the organization is included (or to be included) in the will of a living person ordinarily does not qualify as an unconditional promise to give because living individuals can always change their minds — and their wills.

➥ Organizations that receive pledges must maintain adequate controls over recorded pledges receivable, much the same as commercial enterprises must control their customer accounts receivable, to assure that they are

collected when due. ➝ This means that they should maintain subsidiary ledgers, together with sufficient data about the donor — and the gift — to enable periodic evaluation of these assets and ultimate achievement of this objective. The subsidiary ledger should be reconciled periodically with the general ledger and any differences investigated timely to assure the proper recording in both places of payments received or account adjustments.

There should be a system in place to monitor these receivables that requires contacting the donor timely for collection when they are due, subsequent follow-up if not paid timely, and periodic re-evaluation of the estimated net realizable value to permit fair presentation in the financial statements. In addition, the system should require written approvals at the appropriate levels of authority for any writeoffs or other valuation adjustments to protect the organization against undetected misappropriations or other unrecorded collections.

Organizations that receive conditional pledges should maintain similar controls over them, except that, since they are "unrecorded," they are not reconcilable to the general ledger. Another significant difference is that monitoring activities need to include determining when the condition permitting them to be recorded as revenue and receivables is met.

CHAPTER 9: CASH AND INVESTMENT MANAGEMENT

Cash management. Cash management means getting the maximum use out of your available cash resources. The bank "lockbox" service described in chapter 5, in addition to affording effective control over the recording of cash receipts, is, therefore, also an effective cash management technique.

If substantial cash balances are ordinarily maintained, such as for accumulated reserves (see chapter 4) or scheduled future payouts of obligations (for example, research grants) not likely to be expended soon, separate, interest-bearing accounts (like short-term certificates of deposit "money market" accounts or other high quality, liquid, short term investments) may be employed to balance risk management objectives with interest rate returns and to offset typical bank charges (see below). For larger organizations that have human resources with the skills and time to devote to daily cash management activities, there are any number of more sophisticated short-term investment instruments that may be employed more effectively for this purpose, but that are not discussed here in this limited space because of their rapidly expanding variety and complexity.

Mitigating bank charges. Bank charges can be substantial if your organization has an active account, for example, if you process a high volume of checks for small donations — and especially if you are using a "lockbox" service. However, sometimes, as a public service, smaller banks are willing to waive or limit transactional or other bank charges for not-for-profit organizations operating in their local markets, particularly if one or more of your officers or board members has a relationship with a bank officer. (*CAUTION:* If waived bank charges are significant, however, their value should be estimated and recorded as "in-kind gifts" and offsetting expenses — see chapter 3.)

To enable relatively small organizations to offset bank charges and maximize interest returns with minimal risk tolerance, a "money market" account, preferably with unlimited checking privileges (if available), is recommended. Some financial institutions provide "sweep" services that automatically transfer balances between money market and operating checking accounts, as needed.

↪ *For control purposes, it is best that authorized signers named on "money*

market" or time deposit accounts be fewer than on operating accounts. ↵
When needed, occasional transfers should be made to operating accounts
before disbursing such funds outside the organization. This places these
expenditures under the other normal control procedures for cash
disbursements.

Cash flow forecasting. ↳ *For organizations without the luxury of cash
resources that ordinarily exceed current needs, for example, those typically
operating on a breakeven or near breakeven basis, cash flow forecasting
is an essential element of effective cash management.* ↵ The more
unpredictable the rate of cash inflows from contributions or collections of
fees or pledges (for example when engaged in untried fundraising
campaigns or markets), the more important it becomes to supplement cash
flow forecasts with projections based on hypothetically varied rates of
inflow. This will enable limited cash resources to be expended on a
priority basis and not foolishly invested in long-term instruments with
significant short-term market risk in the face of short-term cash needs. To
achieve this kind of control, it is critical to identify, segregate and prioritize
future cash outflow requirements into fixed and variable or discretionary
categories, and long and short term investible funds. The ideal frequency
of this exercise depends on the degree of uncertainty of cash inflows, and
the level of cash or other liquid reserves ordinarily on hand.

Investments. ↳ *For organizations fortunate (or wise) enough to have
significant investible funds, investment management is usually among the
most formidable of the fiduciary responsibilities of the treasurer and the
board.* ↵ Many organizations often accumulate funds in excess of the
organization's current operating needs for various specified or unspecified
purposes. Sometimes, these funds are in the nature of endowments (see
chapters 6 and 13) and are, therefore, required to be maintained intact
permanently (or for a relatively long time); other times, funds are
accumulated on a relatively short-term or medium-term basis for specific
projects or needs. In these cases, organizations are faced with making
prudent investment decisions beyond their day-to-day cash management
activities to maximize the value of these funds with risk tolerance levels
consistent with their intended purpose and use.

These decisions become more difficult — and more important — the
greater the value of the assets, and the more diversified and complex their
intended purposes. When the value of investible funds and difficulty of
investment decisions reach a certain point, a designated committee of the

board (for example, an investment committee, most likely headed by the treasurer, or the finance committee) should be charged with the responsibility for making such decisions. In smaller organizations, the entire board should take it on.

Many organizations and their boards are fearful of such responsibility and, as a result, tend to make overly conservative and simplistic investment decisions that may not be consistent with results that might be obtained based on more rational and informed deliberations. The result obtained is often that all investible funds, regardless of intended purpose or value, are invested indefinitely in highly liquid and safe, but low yielding, investment instruments, such as certificates of deposit, "money market" accounts and United States Treasury bills or notes. In fact, there have been organizations whose directors or trustees responsible for investing and managing substantial endowments have had to defend themselves in litigation for investing too conservatively. The plaintiffs in such litigation asserted that the investments made were too risk-averse and, thus, severely reduced the ability of the endowment to generate sufficient income to meet its objectives, as expressed or implied by the donor.

In addition, whenever donated investment securities are received, many organizations tend to hold on to the securities indefinitely, without regard to whether such action (or more correctly, inaction) is necessary to comply with the donor's intent or is in any way consistent with an identified and reasonably appropriate investment objective of the organization.

A far more intelligent approach (albeit requiring a substantially greater commitment from volunteer trustees in terms of time and responsibility) would be to develop a set of investment objectives for the organization or for each identifiable fund purpose. Different sets of objectives may be selected for different investment funds or portfolios that are for different purposes, for example, long-term *vs.* medium-term *vs.* short-term needs.

Setting investment objectives. To set appropriate investment objectives, consider, for example:

• What is the fund (principal and income) to be used for?

• How long are the funds likely to be invested before they are needed?

• How much risk is tolerable, consistent with the foregoing time horizon?

59

In substantial part, these concepts constitute the basis of principles of sound investment management by fiduciaries that are both firmly established in law and well known. These principles include the development of an investment policy statement based on identified objectives relating primarily to a time horizon and an appropriate balance of risk tolerance and expected rate of return. Of course, every one would like to minimize risk and maximize return, if they could. But it doesn't work that way because the normal risk/reward relationship is direct, not inverse; the greater the risk, the greater the potential return — and *vice versa.*

Moreover, under such an approach, any donated securities not required by the donor to be retained (a condition that rarely should be acceptable to the organization) should be liquidated and the proceeds reinvested in accordance with the organization's approved investment objectives.

Selecting an investment program, plan or approach. Following the exercise of selecting investment objectives, the investment committee or board then needs to seek and select an investment program or plan that it believes will best meet its objectives.

Among the other established principles of sound investment management are the following:

- Select expert professional investment advisers and managers

- Allow your professional experts to exercise discretion, and have them acknowledge their responsibilities as co-fiduciaries

- Diversify your investments

Monitor the performance of your professionals.

Ordinarily, to achieve most investment objectives (other than, perhaps, minimum risk/maximum liquidity — which generally produces the lowest yield) diversification is necessary.

- **Money management:** The major securities brokerage firms offer investment programs that afford substantial diversification. They are attractive to individuals, businesses and organizations with between $100,000 and $5 million in funds that are investible with common investment objectives because they enable investors to access the services of many of the most accomplished and respected money managers in the country, people whose services are otherwise available only to those with $5-10 million portfolios.

Here's how they work typically:

- Based on performance reviews and continuous monitoring by investment specialists, the brokerage firm evaluates and selects a number of professional, independent money managers to participate in their program.

- Prospective investors complete questionnaires submitting their investment objectives for each portfolio. Portfolios may be divided and allocated among different managers merely to take advantage of additional diversity of investment strategies, all intended to achieve the same or similar objectives. Detailed profiles of the managers are provided to the investor who then selects one for each investment portfolio. Each portfolio is ordinarily subject to a minimum investment, often, $100,000.

- Investor input is fed into a computer that selects investment managers whose stated goals, emphasis, activities and performance results best match the investor's selected objectives.

- A fee is charged to the account periodically based on the value of the portfolio(s), and there are no transaction fees for trades. The rate of return actually earned will vary, of course, based on market cycle factors and based on the investment objectives selected, but are fairly predictable within an acceptable range, based on performance history.

- The account executive at the brokerage firm often provides additional monitoring of the money management firm's performance and, for example, for changes in key personnel or strategies, to see that its investment decisions remain consistent with the selected investment objectives.

These money management programs allow the responsibility for selecting both the investment objectives and the money manager(s) to reside with the investing organization, where it should be, but transfer the responsibility for researching and selecting actual investments (a rather formidable one for members of a volunteer board) to qualified professionals with proven track records, whose sole missions and responsibilities are to meet the investment objectives of their clients.

The cost of these money management programs may seem high in comparison to other plans when viewed in the absence of other considerations. But consider that the fee structure provides additional incentive to the money managers to make investment decisions intended only to maximize the value of the portfolio, rather than to trade for the sake of earning transaction "commissions." And often, discounted rates can be arranged for charitable organizations.

➥ *The right way to select an investment program is to consider your organization's risk tolerance, the expected rate of return — **net** of the costs — and whether such results are likely to be otherwise consistent with its investment objectives.* ➤

Use of professional money managers through these access programs is only one of many ways smaller investors can achieve the benefits of investment diversity and professional management. A few of the other more commonly employed alternatives are discussed below.

- **Mutual funds:** Compare these money manager access programs, for example, to the popular choice of investing in one or more mutual funds. Investment fees associated with mutual funds are paid only once, either at the time of investment (called "load funds") or at the time the investment is sold (called "no-load funds"). Therefore, these investments are less expensive, the longer they are held. You should be aware, however, that there is an additional investment risk associated with most mutual funds. That is that entry into, or withdrawal from, the fund of major investors (for example, large pension plans) may adversely affect the fund's performance independently of that of the market segment it invests in. Such events can require the mutual fund to buy or sell investments at times when market conditions make such action unwise and, therefore, not in the best interests of the other investors in the fund. A money management program carries no such risk and is like having your own mutual fund, and the manager is working for you.

- **Other investment managers:** There are also investment managers that market their services directly to smaller investors of as little as $50,000, often primarily individuals and retirees, and generally at lower fees than the major brokerage firms' programs for accessing the premium quality money managers. While many of these services may be performed by highly qualified individuals, some are not, many have little depth (only one or two key people), and some may be scams. Since these smaller operators rarely provide verifiable statistical performance information or other standard disclosure material such as is used consistently by the more widely known professional firms, their performance and dependability are ordinarily extremely difficult to evaluate with any degree of comfort or assurance. Therefore, it is recommended that they ordinarily be avoided unless a board member has direct knowledge of their honesty, prior performance and competence. Particular care should be taken when the investment manager's marketing material contains rather insupportable or dubious claims such as *"We provide the best investment experience available"* or otherwise has a distinctly amateurish, overall appearance.

• **Community foundations:** Another alternative investment program to consider might be to use a service offered by certain not-for-profit organizations known as "community foundations" or similar organizations. A community foundation's principal purpose ordinarily is to make grants in furtherance of a number of charitable program purposes. Apparently, because many community foundations are blessed with large endowments intended to benefit their programs, they are ordinarily well equipped to manage their own investments. Accordingly, they offer investment management and other administrative services to individuals who find it impractical or inconvenient to set up and manage their own foundations — and to other qualified charitable organizations — by inviting them to pool their investible funds with those of the community foundation.

Not-for-profit organizations that do not have the resources (such as qualified staff or volunteer time) to manage their own investments or that, for whatever reason, do not wish to take on the responsibility, often take advantage of the services of community foundations. Although they may be substantial to the investor organizations, their investible assets are often viewed by the foundations as relatively small. Under such arrangements, the community foundation's investment objectives ordinarily are determined by its own trustees based on its own program goals — not the transferor organization's — and are the same for all participants, with some exceptions.

Also, community foundations generally require that ownership of the investible assets be transferred to the foundation and that it be "trusted" not only to invest them prudently, but to expend the income earned thereon and, sometimes, return or otherwise dispose of the fund principal, in accordance with the instructions of the transferor entities. In marketing these typically informal (and nonbinding) arrangements, the foundations frequently cite as a benefit the fact that the assets are removed from the transferor organization's balance sheet, where, if they remained, they might otherwise impair the effectiveness of its fundraising activities by giving potential donors the impression that the organization is accumulating wealth and, therefore, not in need of a donation.

Therefore, the disadvantages of this type of arrangement include lack of control over such things as the selection of investment objectives and the investment manager or managers and, in fact, over the disposition of the funds' income and principal. When approving a transfer of investible funds to a community or similar foundation under such an arrangement, the transferor organization's board also loses control over significant resources with which it was entrusted and accepts the risk that it will be criticized for doing so and, thereby, accused of abdicating a formidable board responsibility.

- **Bank trust departments:** Trust departments of commercial banks and other financial institutions (for example, insurance companies) offer investment programs similar to community foundations. However, although they may or may not require a transfer of responsibility for investment decisions, they typically do not require the loss of control over disposition of the income. When these trust arrangements involve pooled funds of several investors with similar investment objectives, they are called "collective" (or "common") trust funds.

CHAPTER 10: ROLE AND SELECTION OF INDEPENDENT ACCOUNTANTS

Many organizations are required by their own by-laws or policy, or those of an affiliated central organization, and (depending on the source or amount of money raised) by state or local law or regulation, or contractual agreement, to engage the services of an independent certified public accountant or firm to conduct an audit, review or compilation of, and issue a report on, the organization's annual financial statements. The purpose of an audit or review report is to provide some additional assurance to financial statement users — based on the CPA's independence and professional knowledge and reputation — as to the reliability of the financial statements.

Even though the independent CPA often assists in preparing the financial statements, particularly for smaller reporting entities, the financial statements and accompanying notes are always to be regarded solely as representations of management, not the CPA. The CPA's representations are limited to those contained in the audit, review or compilation report, a letter accompanying the financial statements.

Selecting an independent accountant/auditor. Selecting an independent auditor (or an independent accountant to perform nonaudit services) may be the job of the treasurer or finance committee, or it may be the job of a separate audit committee (see chapter 11).

Regardless of the type of professional services required (see below), because of the highly specialized and complex accounting standards and rules that apply, and the unique risks and other considerations associated with not-for-profit organizations, only an appropriately experienced CPA should be selected, based primarily on professional reputation, as indicated by referrals, and by interview. While it is nice to keep costs to a minimum, fees should never be the sole determinant in the selection.

Audit services. Because of the serious professional responsibility undertaken by an auditor, a substantial amount of time must be expended to do the job right. Unless the auditor is donating, or significantly discounting, his/her professional time because of dedication to your cause (which many are willing to do, if asked), this time is typically expensive.

However, an effective audit is usually money well spent. It not only provides protection for the donors, it is often the best — and the least expensive — way a board of trustees or directors can obtain assurance that it is meeting is formidable fiduciary responsibilities.

Moreover, among the most important secondary functions of the independent auditor are required communications about illegal acts and other accounting auditing, and reporting issues (discussed in chapter 11) and to make practical recommendations for improving the bookkeeping and financial reporting systems to make them more streamlined or more useful and informative and for strengthening the organization's internal controls and other financial management functions. Therefore, when interviewing a prospective auditor, you should establish an understanding that you expect such recommendations as a by-product of his/her services.

As stated in the modern, standard audit report, an audit is designed to permit the auditor to:

> ...obtain *reasonable assurance* about whether the financial statements are *free of material misstatement*. An audit includes examining, *on a test basis*, evidence supporting the amounts and disclosures in the financial statements. An audit also includes assessing the accounting principles used and significant estimates *made by management* [often based on the advice, or with the assistance, of the auditor but, nonetheless, management's responsibility], as well as evaluating the overall financial presentation. [Emphasis added.]

The auditor's report includes the auditor's professional opinion, formed as a result of conducting the audit. The auditor's opinion generally speaks only to whether management's financial statements are presented fairly, *in all material respects*, in conformity with GAAP.

Notice the italicized words in the preceding two paragraphs. It is important to understand that despite its intensive scrutiny, an audit is not foolproof and cannot be expected to catch all misstatements in the financial statements. Auditors do not look at everything; the cost would be prohibitive. In many areas of the audit, they limit their work to tests of samples that, in their professional judgment, are likely to be representative of many transactions and sufficient in scope to identify *material* misstatements, if there are any.

To evaluate the quality of audit work to be expected, you need to determine in advance how many hours the auditor plans to spend (regardless of the fee) and what areas the CPA intends to address as those presenting the most audit risk. The number of audit hours to be spent is directly related to three factors: the quality of the recordkeeping, the effectiveness of internal control and the quality of the audit. You do not want an independent auditor who will take shortcuts to keep fees down.

A quality audit by an experienced and competent auditor of not-for-profit organizations, even for the smallest entity, with books and records in excellent shape and reasonably effective internal control, ordinarily should take *at least* 25-50 hours (and up to many hundreds for larger organizations or those with poorer accounting records or controls), often more if the auditor also will assist in preparing the financial statements. Principal audit risks identified by the auditor should coincide closely with the control objectives and related risks identified by management — if both are doing their jobs right.

Internal control examinations. Independent auditors also may be engaged to perform procedures that constitute an examination enabling them to opine on the operating effectiveness of the organization's internal control. This service (so far) has never been required for (and not commonly obtained by) not-for-profit organizations. However, such an independent assessment can be effective in helping the board or other financial oversight body to meet its fiduciary responsibility by providing comfort to it, as well as to the organization's donors and other constituency, as to the reliability of the organization's financial records and reports.

Review services. Except where audits are required by state or local law or regulation (see chapter 12), or as many do, the organization's governing document (by-laws), for practical cost reasons, smaller organizations are encouraged to engage independent CPAs to perform, in place of an audit, a less intensive and, therefore, less expensive, service called a "review." Sometimes review services are required by state or local law for certain organizations that need not get audits.

For a review service, the CPA (technically, not referred to as an auditor in these circumstances) needs not examine documentary evidence but relies on analytical procedures (that answer questions like, "Do the numbers make sense?") and management inquiries to provide the basis for a report. The independent CPA's review report does not contain an opinion because the scope of the work performed is insufficient to support one. Instead, it contains a more limited form of assurance on the financial statements called "negative" assurance because it is expressed in the negative as follows:

> Based on our review, we are not aware of any material modifications that should be made to the accompanying financial statements for them to be in conformity with generally accepted accounting principles.

Compilation services. An independent CPA may offer also a still less expensive professional service compiling the organization's financial statements in proper form, without performing any procedures intended to enable the CPA to express any assurance on the reliability of the financial information contained therein. Therefore, this limited service results in *no assurance* from the CPA but may be appropriate, nevertheless, for the smallest of organizations. Sometimes compilation services are required by state or local law for certain organizations that need not get audits or reviews.

Other CPA services. Independent CPAs can provide your organization with other services, as well, such as governance consulting, assistance in complying with federal, state and, sometimes local, regulatory reporting requirements (see chapter 12) or any of the other topics covered in this **HANDBOOK**.

It is common for small organizations to use their outside CPAs for routine bookkeeping services, often in conjunction with the compilation of financial statements. However, unless the CPA's practice is geared to offer such services competitively (which many are not), or unless the CPA is donating — or significantly discounting — these services, it is generally more cost effective — because of high hourly billing rates — to limit the CPA's involvement in bookkeeping to assisting in the selection, training and supervision (to the extent necessary) of a qualified part-time bookkeeper (or *per diem* bookkeeping service) engaged directly by the organization.

CHAPTER 11: AUDIT COMMITTEES

The oversight function in the financial management structure is so crucial, it is generally considered the board's responsibility, although it is often delegated to a separate committee of the board that may be called the audit committee. Sometimes the board committee responsible for financial oversight is titled the finance or budget committee, or some other name. Audit or other oversight committees play important roles in both for-profit and not-for-profit organizations.

↜ *While some of the typical duties of audit committees are often handled in smaller not-for-profits by the treasurer,* **oversight** *is the most critical dimension of these duties that a treasurer, who is properly fulfilling his or her role, or another committee with broader duties, may not be able to deliver effectively.* ↜ This is because direct and intimate involvement in the budgeting, recordkeeping and financial reporting functions could impair his, her or their objectivity.

Therefore, a separate audit committee is recommended for larger organizations that handle larger amounts of money and that tend to have larger boards with larger agendas. Otherwise, another financial committee or the board, as a whole, should perform the following duties.

By assuming the oversight function on the board's behalf, and devoting the necessary time and attention to careful analysis of the issues, the audit committee frees up the full board to deal with other matters. Nevertheless, the audit committee must report its activities, findings, recommendations and conclusions to the board periodically, and the board must take responsibility for assuring itself that the audit committee is functioning effectively.

Duties of an audit committee. Although the scope of their activities may address other areas of financial management, among the duties typically performed by audit committees, as a minimum, in connection with their oversight function are:

* Selection of independent auditors,

* Review of audit scope and findings,

- Evaluating internal controls, and

- Review and approval for external distribution of financial statements.

While the treasurer is the organization's principal liaison with its independent auditors, and works most closely with them during the audit the audit committee, or similar oversight committee, if any, or the board, should select, or approve the selection of, the independent auditors or recommend their approval by the board. (Considerations involved in selecting auditors are discussed in chapter 10.)

By meeting with and interviewing the independent auditors, before and after the audit, the audit committee should satisfy itself that the audit will be (or was) conducted in accordance with generally accepted auditing standards and sufficient in scope to address any concerns the committee considers appropriate in the circumstances.

The audit committee should critically review all required communications from the auditors and inquire of them to ascertain how the audit went, for example, whether the independent auditors are sufficiently satisfied with the operating effectiveness of internal control and that any recommendations or findings of the auditors in that regard, as well as regarding any fraudulent or other illegal acts, disagreements with management, and significant audit adjustments or other matters were properly communicated to management the committee and the treasurer, and appropriately addressed by management. Some audit committees may wish to engage the independent auditors to expand their evaluation of internal control beyond the scope ordinarily necessary for the audit sufficiently to enable them to express an opinion on its effectiveness (see "internal control examinations," chapter 10) or otherwise to suit the committee's own special needs or interests.

Before authorizing distribution of the organization's annual financial statements outside the organization, the audit committee ordinarily should obtain, in interviews of the treasurer and the auditors, answers to all questions necessary for it to achieve adequate comfort (reasonable assurance) that the financial statements and accompanying disclosures are:

- Presented in accordance with applicable accounting standards and principles (or if not on the accrual basis, that adequate additional disclosures are made),

- Free of material omissions and other misstatements and,

- Sufficiently clear and understandable by expected users.

The audit committee should consider whether the organization needs an ethical code of conduct, especially if it has employees, to communicate management's commitment to fiscal integrity, ethical behavior and compliance with all applicable laws and regulations — and to communicate its expectation that employees share in that commitment.

Size and make-up of an audit committee. *⊷Audit committees function most efficiently and effectively if their size is kept relatively small, say, three members including a chairperson.⊶*

It is best if the audit committee members are business people or professionals experienced with financial matters and, if possible, knowledgeable about the audit service and process (see chapter 10). When there is a separate audit committee, ordinarily, there should be no common members of the audit and finance committees, but the treasurer should function as a liaison between the two.

⊷It is important not to leave this subject without a reminder that the oversight function is a necessary and critical element in your organization's financial management structure and, should your board decide an audit committee is unnecessary, the board, itself, has to accept the responsibility to perform this function diligently.⊶

CHAPTER 12: COMPLYING WITH REGULATORY REQUIREMENTS

This chapter is about *compliance*.

All not-for-profit organizations have obligations imposed on them by others, including government, and certain donors (chapters 12 and 13). It's the treasurer's job to see that those compliance obligations are met.

IRS reporting. Most people are aware that charitable organizations are generally referred to as "tax-exempt," ordinarily meaning substantially exempt from federal income taxes. Many tax-exempt organizations are likewise exempt from federal unemployment tax and, many state and local taxes, as well, often including real estate and sales taxes.

What many people do not realize is that federal tax exempt status is not automatic; it is available only to organizations whose structure and activities conform to statutory descriptions and ordinarily must be applied for and granted by a "determination letter" from the Internal Revenue Service (IRS). And many also do not realize that, with few exceptions (including those that are classified as religious organizations, principally churches), tax-exempt, charitable organizations have the obligation to file annual information returns (usually Form 990 or 990EZ, or 990PF for private foundations) with the IRS and, in some cases, file tax returns (Form 990T) and pay tax on certain kinds of income called "unrelated business income."

If the organization regularly engages in commercial, business-type activities, and earns income in excess of $1,000 annually from such activity, subject to certain statutory exceptions, it may be liable for a federal tax on "unrelated business income" or UBI, payable with Form 990T. If you think this may be the case, it is often best to consult with your national office, if any, or seek professional advice.

Copies of the application for exemption (Form 1023 or 1024) and the last three annual information returns must be retained on file by the organization and, under new requirements, must ordinarily be provided or made available for public inspection during regular business hours or within 30 days of any written request, without charge other than a reasonable fee for reproduction and mailing. *The penalty for willful* *noncompliance is $5,000 per incident.*

Many local affiliates of national or regional organizations, however, are covered by the central organization's *group exemption*. The benefit of the group exemption is to relieve local affiliates of the obligation to apply for their own exemptions, a difficult, time-consuming and, if professional assistance is obtained, potentially expensive, process. For practical reasons, however, many central organizations do not file combined returns for the group (although some do), and the group exemption does not otherwise relieve the local affiliates of their annual filing obligations, if any. Therefore, it is important to ascertain if your organization is covered by a group exemption and whether it is to be included in a combined information return of the central organization and its affiliates.

Annual reports to the IRS on information returns (for example, on Form 990) are due 4½ months after the organization's fiscal year end. Since most not-for-profit organizations have June 30th fiscal year ends, their Forms 990 (or 990EZ) are ordinarily due every November 15th (unless properly extended), subject to the following exceptions for smaller organizations:

- Organizations up to one year old (at year end) that have received gifts or pledges totaling $37,500 or less during their first fiscal year

- Organizations more than one, but less than three, years old (at year end) with annual "gross receipts" (as defined in IRS instructions — see Glossary, *APPENDIX B* of this **HANDBOOK**) averaging $30,000 or less during their first two fiscal years, and

- Organizations three years old or more (at year end) with annual "gross receipts" (as defined) averaging $25,000 or less during the immediately preceding three fiscal years.

For any year that an annual information return is due, the simplified "Short Form" 990EZ may be substituted for the more complex Form 990 only if your organization's gross receipts (once again, as defined) are less than $100,000 *and* its total assets at year end are less than $250,000. (Form 990 is so complex as to virtually demand specialized software or professional assistance.)

These exceptions notwithstanding, for years when no information return is required, the IRS nevertheless recommends that tax-exempt organizations that receive a filing package from the IRS submit a return anyway merely by attaching the pre-addressed mailing label (containing the organization's name, address and federal tax or employer identification number), indicating that the return is not required (see current edition of the IRS instructions), and affixing an officer's signature. You should also insert your central organization's group exemption number, if any, where indicated on the form.

A federal tax ID number (often referred to as an employer identification number or E.I.N.) should be obtained by filing Form SS-4, regardless of whether the entity has employees and regardless of whether the organization is covered by a group exemption, although some central organizations will file the SS-4 for their new affiliates. The E.I.N. is used for all federal tax and information reporting purposes, including payroll taxes, and may be used for certain state or local governmental reporting purposes, as well.

➥Penalties for failure to file required returns, or filing of incomplete or incorrect returns, increase on a daily basis and can be substantial — ordinarily up to $10,000 per year for the organization (or $50,000 for larger organizations with more than $1 million in annual gross receipts) and up to $5,000 personally for each responsible party, plus, if there is any unpaid, unreported UBI tax, up to 25% of the tax due for late or nonfiling and an additional 25% for late or nonpayment —plus interest.➥

The IRS requires tax-exempt organizations, among others, to file certain other information returns on a calendar year basis (principally, on Form 1099-MISC, but there are others) reporting certain types of payments, prizes and awards to individuals, unincorporated businesses and incorporated law firms, and sometimes withholding income taxes. Gambling winnings (for example, if your organization runs a bingo game or Las Vegas night) are reportable on Form W-2G. Failure to file these information returns timely and correctly, as required, without reasonable cause, may cause *penalties of up to $50 per return*.

The law places a burden on not-for-profit organizations to provide donors with a brief written statement of the good-faith estimate of the value (unless nominal) of any privileges or benefits (goods or services) provided to the donor as an incentive or in exchange for any donation in excess of $75.

For a donor to be entitled to an income tax deduction for any contribution of $250 or more, the donor must have received a receipt from the charity that also describe the gift, in addition to disclosing the value of any privileges or benefits received by the donor as an incentive or in exchange for the gift, even if less than $75. Although the law places the burden on the donor — not the charity — to obtain the receipt (in support of the deduction) for gifts valued at $250 or more, not-for-profit organizations generally provide them automatically as a matter of good donor relations. In the case of a conditional gift, the organization may wish to inform the donor that the gift might not be deductible until the condition is met. (This sometimes results in the removal of the condition.) Moreover, if the gift is for property, it is also the donor/taxpayer's obligation to establish its value — not the charity's — even though, as discussed in chapter 3, generally accepted accounting principles require the organization to establish and record a value anyway for financial reporting purposes. (The value used by the organization for financial reporting purposes need not be the same as that used by the donor for income tax reporting purposes.)

It is not necessary to aggregate multiple gifts given in the same year for purposes of either of the foregoing two requirements.

Lobbying. Historically, Congress and the IRS have viewed significant lobbying activities as inconsistent with most exemptions from income taxes under Internal Revenue Code (IRC) Section (§) 501(c). Accordingly, the tax exemptions of such organizations whose activities were found to involve any type of lobbying activity in "substantial part" were at risk. To complicate matters, under old law, "substantial part" was neither defined nor determined based on dollars expended (but also considered expenditures of volunteer hours, which are rarely recorded or otherwise objectively measurable). It was left largely up to an examining IRS agent to decide subjectively when the rule was violated.

Nevertheless, over the last couple of decades, not-for-profit organizations concerned with issues of public health and social welfare have found it increasingly critical to the achievement of their missions to engage in advocacy programs that seek to influence legislation or public opinion. In recognition and response to this need, many years ago, Congress enacted §501(h) of the IRC, known as the "Lobbying Safe Harbor Rule." Nevertheless, substantial lobbying activities in regard to partisan politics (for example, those that are directed toward the election or defeat of specific candidates for public office) remain prohibited even under §501(h).

Under §501(h), lobbying activity by public charities (not private foundations) exempt under §501(c)(3) that is intended to influence legislation or public opinion is permitted, subject to two rather generous limitations, including:

1. The "nontaxable limit" on allowable lobbying expenditures (the excess over which are subjected to a 25% excise tax) is 25% of the organization's "exempt purpose expenditures." ("Exempt purpose expenditures" for this purpose are equal to total expenditures, less fundraising expenditures.)

2. The overall limitation on legislative activity for loss of exemption purposes is 150% (*i.e.*, lobbying expenses must be at least 150% of the nontaxable limit or, in other words, 37.5% of total exempt purpose expenditures). However, the 150% test is applied based only on four-year cumulative amounts, including pre-election years.

Therefore, to risk loss of its income tax exemption, an organization would have to violate this test consistently (on the average) — *over a four-year period*. Indeed, this is a pretty safe harbor to swim in. (Theoretically, under this limitation, an organization could spend 100% of its available resources in a single year on allowable lobbying activities, and not risk loss of exemption if it refrained from such activity for the next three years.)

To take advantage of §501(h), the organization's accounting system must track and summarize expenditures for allowable lobbying activities. In addition, a formal election must be made with IRS; otherwise, the old law will apply. A §501(h) election, however, is virtually risk free because, in the unlikely event that it would ever become disadvantageous to retain it, it is revocable (prospectively) with a single stroke of the pen when filing a subsequent 990.

You might also wish to know this. ← *The IRS has announced publicly that the mere making of a §501(h) election enabling lobbying activity will not trigger an audit.* → On the contrary, if you engage in legislative activities and do not make the election, your organization would be required to describe its lobbying activities in its annual 990s, and report the related expenditures, including an allocation of staff time, and certain information about volunteer lobbying. Without the safe harbor of a §501(h) election, the reporting of such activities would appear to be far more likely to invite an audit — and the risk of some serious trouble.

According to The Bureau of National Affairs (BNA), "leading authorities generally recommend that the election be made by any §501(c)(3) organization that engages 'even remotely in efforts to influence legislation or public opinion...'. The election provides a relatively certain, objective, and generous yardstick based on expenditures alone, in an otherwise murky area. ... This is a significant improvement over the [older alternative] substantial part test, which can be triggered by volunteer activity."

On the other hand, if your organization engages in this type of activity, and you want an IRS agent to decide its future by subjectively estimating how "substantial" such activity is, don't make the §501(h) election.

State and local regulatory requirements. Just about every state requires charities that raise funds in that state to register and make annual reports, usually to the state Attorney General's office. In fact, many regulations applicable to fundraising from the general public include requirements for public, written financial and other disclosures, often with particular attention to allocations of costs associated with fundraising to other functional activities (see chapter 3). Even public appeals for volunteer services are often subject to regulation. Some states, and some local governments, require reports to other agencies, as well, and all requirements carry penalties for noncompliance. To be sure the organization is in compliance, the treasurer must carefully ascertain, — every year — what these requirements are. Here again, seeking professional advice or help from your central organization's staff is recommended.

Grant compliance. As discussed in chapter 6, government grants generally come packaged with a number of statutory, regulatory and contractual compliance requirements. Failure to comply with these requirements, among other possible penalties, may result in a liability to return grant funds even after they have been dispensed in good faith. This requires that someone in the organization be familiar with all applicable grant compliance requirements, and monitor compliance.

Other requirements. If you are an affiliate of a central organization (with or without a group exemption), the central organization probably requires submission of timely and accurate financial reports periodically.

Compliance with the requirements of donors regarding restricted contributions to the organization and pass-through donations to other organization (agency transactions) is discussed in chapter 13.

CHAPTER 13: DONOR RESTRICTIONS AND AGENCY TRANSACTIONS

Once again, accountability is a fundamental component of any financial management structure, the bricks and mortar upholding the public trust.

► *One of the most significant features of the accountability obligations that must be accepted by charities and other not-for-profit organizations is their accountability to those who provide their resources.* ◄

When a charity accepts a contribution from a donor who communicates the intended use of his/her donation, it creates a binding contract with, and an obligation of accountability to, the donor as to the proper use of those funds. For substantial gifts, it is best to have any donor restrictions and other terms of the gift committed to writing, including, if it is a pledge, when it is expected to be paid, to reduce the opportunity for misunderstanding and noncompliance, and to assure proper accounting for the gift. Endowments (discussed below and in chapter 6) are special contributions that ordinarily cannot be spent by the recipient; instead, the recipient is permitted to invest these funds and use only the investment income they generate.

As discussed in chapter 3, it is best to use fund accounting, or establish other bookkeeping controls, rather than use separate, special-purpose bank accounts, to assure the proper use of restricted net assets or funds. Proper accounting for restricted funds and their use is another area where the treasurer, if not an accountant, may benefit from some professional help. The most serious risk regarding donor restrictions, however, is the risk that the restriction will go unnoticed and, therefore, unrecorded, thus making it difficult, if not impossible, to comply with the donor's wishes.

It is probably impractical in most small, volunteer organizations to have someone double-check all donor communications accompanying their donations. But remember, the objective of internal control is reasonable — not absolute — assurance, as to the absence of material — not all — misstatements. Therefore, the risk of unrecorded donor restrictions can be satisfactorily mitigated by requiring review of donor communications relating only to donations over a certain value to obtain reasonable assurance that any restrictions have been recorded. The audit or other financial oversight committee, or the board, ordinarily should determine the threshold for review. These reviews should be made periodically by the treasurer or other individual not involved with the initial recording of the donation.

Endowment funds. Not-for-profit organizations often receive assets with donor stipulations that they be held either in perpetuity, indefinitely until certain objectives are achieved, or for a specified time certain. During this holding time, only the income from the investment of such funds may be expended — often for a donor-designated purpose but, occasionally, at the discretion of the organization or its board. These are commonly called endowments or endowment funds. The portion of the endowment that is required to remain intact permanently, or for the donor-specified period, is called the endowment *"corpus"* or "principal," and the expendable portion of the endowment funds is called endowment "income." It is not always clear what constitutes endowment *corpus vs.* income, and that is discussed below.

When endowment *corpus* is required by the donor to remain intact in perpetuity they are, of course, called "permanent endowments" and classified for financial reporting purposes as permanently restricted. This is the most common form of endowment. All other endowment *corpus* (referred to as "term endowments"), and all unexpended endowment income and other funds that are restricted to use for a donor-specified purpose, are classified as temporarily restricted. Of course, unexpended endowment income that may be used at the discretion of the organization or its board is classified as unrestricted.

Also classified as unrestricted are funds that function as endowments because they have been designated by the organization's governing board, rather than by a donor, for use only for special purposes. These are called board-designated "quasi-endowments." They are unrestricted net assets or funds, because in this context, by definition, only a donor can impose, revise or release a restriction (short of making expenditures in compliance therewith). By way of contrast, a board designation, on the other hand, can be reversed by subsequent vote of the board.

Unless specified by the donor, it is necessary often to determine whether realized and unrealized gains on investments should be treated as endowment income or *corpus* by reference to — and interpretation (often difficult and subject to disagreement among lawyers) of — state law. In the absence of donor-imposed or legal requirements to characterize them as *corpus*, gains and losses are accounted for as endowment income and classified as additions to temporarily restricted or unrestricted net assets, depending on the presence or absence of temporary restrictions imposed by the donor.

Although historically, endowed organizations were advised to follow trust law in making such determinations, which treated gains as *corpus*, beginning in 1972, most states have adopted statutes governing how endowments are to be managed. These newer statutes are in substantial conformity with model legislation called the Uniform Management of Institutional Funds Act (UMIFA).

UMIFA, in its original, unaltered form, is essentially permissive, not restrictive. It does not require that investment gains (or losses) be retained and classified as *corpus* but (in the absence of a donor specification to the contrary), places the burden on the organization's governing board to determine what spending policies and practices relative to both realized and unrealized investment gains, are prudent in the circumstances. The board is required to consider such factors as the purpose of the endowment, its expected short-term and long-term financial requirements and investment return, including economic conditions and trends. In fact, it is imprudent and inconsistent with a board's fiduciary responsibility under UMIFA to defer indefinitely and never address the expenditure of some appropriate portion of the investment return consistent with the endowment's purpose.

Consider how a rigid requirement to treat investment gains as inviolable *corpus* could result in the manipulative selection of investment instruments based solely on whether they produce expendable income (interest and dividends) rather than asset appreciation, without any substantive regard to whether the choices under consideration are likely to meet investment objectives more appropriate in the circumstances.

For substantial endowments, it is recommended that the board consider setting aside — and keeping invested — a portion of the unexpended endowment income (determined by applying a regional or national inflation rate) to supplement the *corpus* for the purpose of equalizing the purchasing or earning power of the invested funds. Reserves so set aside retain the same character as temporarily restricted or unrestricted as other unexpended income of the respective funds and should not be reclassified to match the classification of the *corpus*. Just as for board-designated, unrestricted funds, actions by the board to set aside such funds are reversible, for example, based on changing conditions, subject to compliance with the UMIFA requirement to exercise appropriate prudence.

Agency transactions and obligations. Agency (or custodian) transactions result in obligations and special funds used to account for resources received and held by not-for-profit organizations as an agent or intermediary for donors or other resource providers who have directed that those resources be transferred to specified third-party recipients. The intermediary organization has little or no discretion over the use of those resources. Accounting for agency transactions and obligations, and distinguishing agency transactions from contributions are discussed in chapter 3. Because the assets and liabilities associated with these agency funds are always equal, there are no net assets to be reported. Although funds received in agency transactions are not treated for financial reporting purposes as restricted contributions and net assets, nevertheless, they require similar accountability to the resource providers, as well as the intended ultimate recipient entity. Therefore, to reasonably assure compliance, they should be subjected to similar controls.

CHAPTER 14: HUMAN RESOURCE MANAGEMENT

This chapter highlights matters that relate primarily to organizations that have employees and, to a more limited extent, those that engage independent contractors in lieu of employees.

Human resource management policies. ↜*A positive attitude, a spirit of teamwork and a common sense of mission and direction among staff are necessary to avoid conflicts between management and staff, or among staff, and to promote employee satisfaction and efficient operations.*↝ Consequently, the need for communicating clear, written policies on a variety of human resource management issues to all employees — so there is no confusion among staff as to the subject matter — increases proportionately to the size of the staff. Human resource policies are usually contained in a personnel manual that is distributed to all employees.

The adoption, dissemination and consistent observance of human resource policies often afford employers effective protection against lawsuits from employees for unfair or otherwise improper treatment (including wrongful termination), which lawsuits can be expensive. Such lawsuits are more prevalent in some states or areas than in others, for example, California, where it is recommended that policies be reviewed and approved, prior to adoption, by legal counsel knowledgeable in such matters, or another qualified human resource professional.

An organization's human resource policy manual ordinarily should contain its organization chart, mission statement and an ethical code of conduct with a series of standards of behavior, for example, a conflicts of interests policy, and others with regard to the fundraising (see chapter 6) and the financial reporting process (see chapter 3) functions. The National Society of Fund Raising Executives' "Statements of Ethical Principles" is an excellent source of material for ethical standards about fundraising, and the "Standards in Philanthropy" of the National Charities Information Bureau (discussed in chapters 3 and 4) is an excellent source of material for ethical standards about financial reporting.

In addition, the Institute of Management Accountants (IMA) has issued "Standards of Ethical Conduct for Practitioners of Management Accounting and Financial Management," intended for employees engaged in the financial reporting function. These standards may be applied with equal relevance to "independent contractors" (see below) and volunteers — including treasurers. They deal with the subjects of competence, confidentiality, integrity and objectivity. Most significantly, however, they afford guidance as to how to resolve ethical conflicts about financial reporting issues with others in the organization. The IMA can be reached at 800/638-4427 or 201/573-9000 (www.rutgers.edu/ accounting/raw/ima).

Some other examples of the significant topics typically covered by human resource policies include:

- Anti-discrimination and harassment policies

- Employee benefits

- Position descriptions, performance evaluation, salary review and advancement criteria and procedures

- Expense reimbursement procedures

- Office hours and standards of dress and office decorum

A prototype human resource policy manual designed to help not-for-profit organizations develop their own is available from the Center for Nonprofit Management (CNM). (In addition to its written form, it is provided also in electronic form to facilitate editing to suit the organization.) CNM provides educational services, consultation, and information to help not-for-profit organizations and can be reached at 615/259-0100 (www.cnm.org).

There are also a number of inexpensive software packages available in retail outlets that can be used to select and draft human resource policies and create a personnel manual for your organization, for example, *Policies Now* and *Employee Manual Maker*.

Officer/director compensation. The question often arises as to whether it is all right to offer fees or other compensation to officers and directors or trustees, particularly following the William Aramony matter discussed at the beginning of this **HANDBOOK**.

In deciding such questions, it should be noted that one of the conditions for obtaining (and retaining) tax exempt status is that no income generated by the organization may inure to any individual. And the Internal Revenue Service (IRS) is now empowered to impose sanctions in response to perceived excessive executive compensation or conflicts of interests. ☛ *Therefore, extreme care is advised in setting the compensation level of highly paid executives, and it is ordinarily best to maintain conflicts of interest policies for executive staff and board members, preferably including one that precludes board members from being compensated in any way for services rendered to the organization (unless it is considered absolutely necessary in the circumstances).* ☚

The issue — which can be controversial — is discussed in a statement issued in December 1989 by the Board of Directors of the Council on Foundations, entitled "Compensation of Directors and Trustees." It appears on pp. 285-287 in the *Handbook on Private Foundations* (Revised Edition), by David F. Freeman and the Council on Foundations (the Foundation Center, New York, NY, 1991). Although the Statement does not speak directly to compensation of executive staff, who are often officers but not often directors or trustees, it stated wisely (more than two years before the Aramony matter) that "[e]ven the perception of excessive compensation can be damaging to the whole field of philanthropy."

As to directors or trustees, in consideration of the arguments in both directions, the statement issuers pointed out that, under federal law (and that of many states), payment of compensation to directors is legally permissible if not excessive or unreasonable. They further observed that in assessing the reasonableness of such compensation, organizations should consider the nature of the services to be compensated, the skills required, the organization's ability to attract individuals qualified to perform the services, and the time necessary to perform them. Their ultimate conclusion, however, included this admonition. ☛ *Compensation based on an organization's assets or income was not appropriate, and it is **generally** preferable to engage outside professionals, rather than board members, to perform specific (for example, legal), compensated services.* ☚

Use of independent contractors. By the language contained therein, the Council on Foundation's statement technically does not apply to compensating commercial enterprises (such as banks and professional firms) owned by directors or trustees that provide services to organizations. However, there appears to be no logical justification why the same basic legal principle (that is, that such compensation, if any, should be neither excessive nor unreasonable) should not likewise be applied.

In addition, many not-for-profit organizations, particularly the smaller ones, engage and classify individual staff workers as independent contractors to avoid the administrative burdens and costs (*i.e.*, taxes and benefits) of maintaining a payroll. However, the IRS has viewed such arrangements negatively for some time and will often seek to change them to employee relationships if the organization's returns are selected for audit. There are certain tests the IRS will apply to make their determination, the objective of which will be to assess the degree of control exercised by the organization over the worker(s). The greater the control factor, the more likely the IRS is to assert employee status and assess the employer taxes for the period under audit and subsequent periods. Often, it is easier to attract and retain, as well as control the activities of, staff if they have employee status. ➤ *Accordingly, the use of independent contractors as staff in lieu of employees should be approached with care and professional advice.* ◄

An effective and practical way to avoid the administrative burdens associated with payroll are to obtain the services of firms offering what is commonly called "employee leasing." Employee leasing arrangements are available at reasonable cost in most cities. Under such arrangements, the "lessor" firm provides the organization's employees and performs all the administrative functions, such as preparing payroll tax forms, and pays all benefits and taxes. The organization ("lessee") is billed for the employees based on an agreed hourly rate that covers all these costs and a small profit for the lessor.

Retirement plans. Like for-profit enterprises, not-for-profit organizations have to compete to attract and retain the best employees. Doing so successfully often requires providing, or enabling employees to provide, for their retirement. Although there are hybrid variations, tax-deferred retirement plans are generally classified in two major categories, "defined benefit" (or "pension") plans and "defined contribution" (often called "profit-sharing") plans. In both categories, employees are not taxed on the amount of the employer or employee contributions into such plans until distributed. They have the following characteristics:

- **Defined benefit plans** require employers to set aside resources in amounts actuarially determined to be sufficient to provide for a contractually obligated benefit level to participating employees upon retirement. Defined benefit plans are funded solely by employer contributions, are non-discretionary once agreed to and, therefore, quite expensive. For these reasons, they are relatively rare in the not-for-profit world except among the strongest organizations, financially.

- **Defined contribution plans** generally allow employers substantially more flexibility as to when and whether to make contributions and how much, although they often carry employer commitments to match employee contributions. Accordingly, they are the most popular among smaller for-profit and not-for-profit organizations.

Until recently, the only defined contribution plans that have been available under federal law to tax exempt organizations are called §403(b) plans (named for the enabling section of the IRC). Beginning in 1998, tax exempt organizations are also permitted to establish §401(k) plans (similarly named) for their employees. Both types permit employees to set aside limited portions of their earnings, thus reducing their currently taxable income, to be invested tax free and distributed (and taxed) following retirement. Both types may be funded solely by employee contributions, but they may permit employers to agree to match portions of or, at their discretion, to contribute in excess of, employee contributions, also subject to certain limitations.

The principal difference between the two types of plans is the nature of the investments that can be made with the funds. Contributions to a §403(b) plan must be used to purchase annuity contracts from insurance companies — very conservative investments. These investments are substantially risk-free, and the tax deferred investment income modest and contractually fixed. On the other hand, contributions to a §401(k) plan may be invested in one or more of an almost unlimited variety of mutual funds or other marketable securities with varying risk levels and commensurate potential investment returns selected by each employee participant to meet his or her investment objectives and needs.

CHAPTER 15: RECORDS MANAGEMENT

Records management has grown to be a monumental challenge of modern times, not just for businesses, but for individuals and volunteer organizations, as well. The primary concerns discussed in this chapter are security and retention.

Security. The most important documents that require physical safeguards are best stored off premises, protected from fire and moisture, such as in a bank vault, with duplicates retained on premises if referred to frequently. An alternative (although less protective) storage place would be fireproof file cabinets. Internally generated electronic media (computer) files* should be backed up frequently to protect against loss of data, with the back-up copies stored separately from those in daily use, and away from electric motors, televisions and other magnetic fields.

Other controls necessary to provide physical and other safeguards over electronic data and the software that processes that data are ordinarily classified in one of four major categories and typically designed to meet control objectives, as follows:

1. **Access:** Access to hardware and software, including program and data files, is restricted only to authorized personnel. (This ordinarily is accomplished through the use of passwords and physical locks on the computers or the rooms that they are kept in.)

2. **Application development and maintenance:** Program modifications are designed to meet the users needs, documented, tested, implemented and approved by users; purchased software is evaluated, customized

---

*   **A word about the "Y2K issue" or "millennium bug:"** Many computerized systems, including both hardware and software applications, use only two digits, rather than four, to record the year in a date field. These systems may recognize the year 2000 (which is entered into the computer as "00") as the year 1900 or some other date, resulting in errors when the dates are used in computations and comparisons. Such problems are characterized collectively as the year 2000 (or either the "Y2K issue" or "millennium bug"). The effects of the Y2K issue on operations and financial reporting may range from minor errors to catastrophic systems failure. It is management's responsibility — and probably the treasurer's — to see that the Y2K issue is satisfactorily addressed. If you are reading this in 1999, get professional help for this one — and soon.

and implemented with appropriate user and management involvement, and new application systems (developed in-house) are appropriately designed, tested, documented and implemented.

3. **Computer operations:** Computer operations are properly staffed, supervised and monitored, and adequate backup and recovery procedures exist in case of a system failure.

4. **Organizational:** The information systems (IS) department or function is organized to provide for segregation of duties between operators, programmers and other IS personnel, and it is independent of user departments.

Records retention. ☛ *There are no hard and fast retention rules for most records.* ☚ On the contrary, with few exceptions, it is largely a matter of good judgment, legal and other and practical considerations. Some key factors to consider in deciding how long to keep certain documents, electronic data files, or other records are the relative importance of their retention (or disposition) for purposes of:

- Establishing compliance with any federal, state or local laws and regulatory requirements

- Documenting the organization's historical development and achievements

- Preventing volunteers and paid staff from wasting precious time rummaging for important documents

- Reducing or preventing unnecessary occupancy costs for storage

- Defending against or pursuing any possible future legal claims.

Following are practical guidelines in the form of recommended retention periods for written and electronic media records common to small, voluntary organizations. ☛ *These guidelines should be used only in conjunction with your own good judgment and experience. When there is any doubt as to a particular document, a good rule-of-thumb is to **keep it** until you have consulted with an attorney, or for tax or financial items, an accountant.* ☚

RECOMMENDED RECORDS RETENTION SCHEDULE

Retain Permanently

- Corporate minutes, charter, bylaws and amendments

- Organizational charter (issued by a central organization) and related documents

- Original application for federal income tax exemption (Form 1023 or 1024) and all documents evidencing federal, state and local tax exempt status

- Year-end financial statements (with accompanying accountants' reports)

- Books of account

- Federal information (Form 990, 990EZ or 990PF) and unrelated business income tax (Form 990T) returns and state and local annual reports and registrations

- Payroll tax returns

Retain Indefinitely

- Executory contracts (where all obligations of parties have not yet been met)

- Donor and membership database records of active donors/members

Retain for Six Years

- Donor/membership records (after last donation)

- Payroll and personnel records (other than payroll tax returns)

- Fiscal year end bank statements and reconciliations

RECOMMENDED RECORDS
RETENTION SCHEDULE (CONTINUED)

Retain for Three Years

- Auditors' recommendations ("management letters")

- Interim financial statements and reports

- Executed contracts (including expired leases and insurance policies)

- Bank statements and reconciliations (except for fiscal year end) and all cancelled checks

- Sales and purchase invoices and supporting documentation (including petty cash vouchers)

- Expense reimbursement reports and supporting documentation

- Other detailed records supporting federal, state and local regulatory reports

- Donor correspondence regarding large donations (whether restricted or not)

- Other important correspondence

- Anything not specifically listed here but considered relatively important

Retain for One Year

- Donor remittance advices (except those accompanying large donations)

- Duplicate bank deposit slips

- Unimportant correspondence

CHAPTER 16: FINDING HELP

Recruiting volunteer professionals for the board. While many volunteer treasurers are, in fact, accountants, the author has tried to make the preceding chapters sufficiently clear and uncomplicated to be used with relative ease and effectiveness, not only by accountants, but by treasurers who are previously unschooled in such matters.

However, having a professional accountant, and other business professionals, such as lawyers and bankers, on the organization's board — serving as members of, or chairing, its finance or audit committee — is, again, like chicken soup. That's right, *it couldn't hurt!* There is no substitute for experience. ↪*If your organization board's composition is lacking in professional talent, you might be surprised at how easy this is to fix.*↩

Accountants and other business professionals are among the most active community service volunteers in this, the leading nation of the world for volunteerism. They have long recognized the value of such service in building recognition and visibility as community leaders.

Most likely, there are any number of board members who know such professionals (or their friends or relatives), who would welcome the opportunity to serve on your organization's board — or just consult with it and offer their advice — if asked to.

Older, more seasoned professionals may regretfully decline your invitation because their volunteer plates are already filled. However, don't give up. Ask them to recommend younger associates or colleagues, and you will usually get a more favorable response. Younger professionals are often looking for opportunities to fine-tune — and show off — their leadership skills.

Other sources of help. If your organization is affiliated with a larger, central organization, the central organization is probably set up to provide significant and valuable advice and assistance to its smaller affiliates.

Other excellent sources of volunteer expertise are your local professional societies and associations, and national organizations and their local affiliates, for example, like Accountants for the Public Interest (API). Through API, volunteer accountants donate their time and expertise to assist small charities, businesses and others. It also publishes a series of guidebooks to assist volunteers to manage these entities. To learn more about API and its volunteer services or publications, call 410/837-6533.

Although its focus is primarily on small business, another source of volunteer assistance is the Service Corps of Retired Executives (SCORE) SCORE has over 12,000 volunteers in approximately 400 chapters located across the U.S. and Puerto Rico. Contact SCORE (at 800/634-0245 to find its counseling location nearest you, or access its website at www.score.org.

A wealth of inexpensive (and uncomplicated) published guidance on not-for-profit governance can be obtained from the National Center for Nonprofit Boards (NCNB). NCNB seeks to improve the effectiveness of not-for-profit organizations by strengthening their governing boards. NCNB also offers membership to not-for-profit leaders. Contact NCNB at 800/883-6262, 202/452-6262 or FAX 202/ 452-6299, or access its website at www.ncnb.org.

A couple of extremely useful and highly recommended periodicals are listed below; they are available by subscription, and informative highlights can be accessed on their websites. Although the first focuses primarily in the fundraising area, both cover financial and other management topics quite extensively. You can also find ads for insurance agencies, software vendors and others offering products specifically for not-for-profit organizations on their pages. They are:

- The Chronicle of Philanthropy
  800/728-2819 (U.S. only) or 740/382-3322
  www.philanthropy.com

- The NonProfit Times
  973/734-1700
  www.nptimes.com

See also the selected bibliography at *APPENDIX C* of this **HANDBOOK**.

APPENDIX A: ILLUSTRATIVE GENERAL-PURPOSE FINANCIAL STATEMENTS

IMAGINARY DISEASES FOUNDATION
STATEMENT OF FINANCIAL POSITION

As of June 30, 1999, with summarized comparative
financial information as of June 30, 1998

ASSETS	1999	1998
Cash and cash equivalents	$ 2,320,362	$ 959,981
Investment in marketable securities	320,772	316,637
Pledges receivable, net of discount and allowance for doubtful collections	680,228	924,495
Prepaid expenses	16,203	21,057
Furniture, equipment and leasehold improvements, less accumulated depreciation of $203,675 in 1999	78,748	117,437
Other assets	18,171	22,012
	$ 3,434,484	$ 2,361,619

LIABILITIES AND NET ASSETS		
Liabilities:		
Grants payable	$ 193,352	$ 46,398
Accounts payable and accrued expenses	83,213	81,722
Agency obligations	50,000	30,000
Deferred rent obligations	167,575	182,513
	494,140	340,633
Net assets:		
Unrestricted	866,696	522,357
Temporarily restricted	1,848,856	1,288,055
Permanently restricted	224,792	210,574
	2,940,344	2,020,986
	$ 3,434,484	$ 2,361,619

See notes to financial statements.

IMAGINARY DISEASES FOUNDATION
STATEMENT OF ACTIVITIES

For the year ended June 30, 1999, with summarized comparative
financial information for the year ended June 30, 1998_____

	Unrestricted	Temporarily Restricted	Permanently Restricted	Total 1999	1998
REVENUES					
Contributions	$ 971,424	$ 1,339,029		$2,310,453	$1,929,486
Bequests	685,155	135,570	$ 14,218	834,943	960,500
Federated campaigns	189,636			189,636	199,529
Investment return	67,139	20,058		87,197	82,062
Special events income	63,437			63,437	62,015
Less special events direct benefit costs	(43,503)			(43,503)	(41,113)
	1,933,288	1,494,657	14,218	3,442,163	3,192,479
EXPENSES					
Program activities:					
Research	784,853			784,853	808,913
Patient services	870,840			870,840	856,212
Public and professional education	319,730			319,730	257,807
	1,975,423			1,975,423	1,922,932
Fundraising	297,066			297,066	354,251
Administration	250,316			250,316	262,762
	2,522,805			2,522,805	2,539,945
Excess of revenues over expenses (expenses over revenues)	(589,517)	1,494,657	14,218	919,358	
Net assets released from restrictions	933,856	(933,856)			
INCREASE IN NET ASSETS	344,339	560,801	14,218	919,358	652,534
Net assets:					
Beginning of year	522,357	1,288,055	210,574	2,020,986	1,368,452
End of year	$ 866,696	$ 1,848,856	$ 224,792	$2,940,344	$2,020,986

See notes to financial statements

96

IMAGINARY DISEASES FOUNDATION
STATEMENT OF CASH FLOWS

For the year ended June 30, 1999, with summarized comparative
financial information for the year ended June 30, 1998_____

	1999	1998
CASH FLOWS FROM OPERATING ACTIVITIES:		
Net cash provided (used) by operating activities	$ 1,328,654	($ 50,819)
CASH FLOWS FROM INVESTING ACTIVITIES:		
Purchase of equipment	(1,729)	(54,239)
Purchase of investment securities	(7,758)	(243,016)
Sale or redemption of investment securities	41,214	380,622
Net cash provided by investing activities	31,727	83,367
NET INCREASE IN CASH AND CASH EQUIVALENTS	1,360,381	32,548
CASH AND CASH EQUIVALENTS:		
Beginning of year	959,981	927,433
End of year	$ 2,320,362	$ 959,981

See notes to financial statements.

97

IMAGINARY DISEASES FOUNDATION
STATEMENT OF FUNCTIONAL EXPENSES

For the year ended June 30, 1999, with summarized comparative
financial information for the year ended June 30, 1998

	Program activities			Supporting activities		Total	
	Research	Patient Services	Education	Fundraising	Administration	1999	1998
Grant awards	$ 688,568	$ 229,060				$ 917,628	$ 1,045,390
Salaries, temporary help and related expenses	40,842	373,610	$ 178,446	$ 76,642	$ 162,445	831,985	701,522
Printing	3,304	34,473	58,719	123,738	1,388	221,622	207,968
Professional fees and other contract services	910	7,390	2,732	7,032	27,918	45,982	73,523
Postage and shipping	1,705	31,265	28,122	45,833	1,786	108,711	87,447
Rent	6,845	58,203	24,496	15,093	28,538	133,175	176,288
Travel and conferences	37,161	60,335	10,539	10,672	5,226	123,933	130,553
Telephone	1,601	39,523	4,069	2,401	2,001	49,595	44,333
Office supplies	566	6,826	2,842	1,464	2,967	14,665	12,038
Miscellaneous	1,330	12,371	2,490	9,745	9,155	35,091	25,891
Depreciation	2,021	17,784	7,275	4,446	8,892	40,418	34,992
	$ 784,853	$ 870,840	$ 319,730	$ 297,066	$ 250,316	$2,522,805	$ 2,539,945

See notes to financial statements.

1. **Description of activities and summary of significant accounting policies:**

Activities. The principal purpose of Imaginary Diseases Foundation (the "Organization") is to fund research directed at finding the cause and cure for a number of identified imaginary diseases. In addition, through its other programs, the Organization provides services to patients suffering from imaginary diseases and their families, it disseminates informative literature and presents educational public awareness programs and scientific symposiums for health care professionals, and it awards grants to fund certain activities of clinics serving the needs of patients with imaginary diseases.

The Organization is a not-for-profit, voluntary health organization exempt from federal income taxes under Section 501(c)(3) of the Internal Revenue Code and classified collectively as a publicly supported charitable organization under Section 509(a)(1). It qualifies for the maximum charitable contribution deduction by donors under Section 170(b)(1)(A)(vi) of the Code.

Basis of presentation. For comparative purposes, certain summarized 1998 information is presented in the financial statements. However, the 1998 information presented does not include sufficient detail to constitute a presentation in conformity with generally accepted accounting principles. Accordingly, readers may wish to refer to the Organization's prior year's audited financial statements from which the summarized information was derived.

Timely preparation of financial statements in conformity with generally accepted accounting principles requires estimates by management, some of which may require revision in future periods.

Cash equivalents and investments. Cash equivalents are defined as money market funds and all other highly liquid investments with original maturities of three months or less. Other investments are carried at fair value based on current market quotes. Realized and unrealized gains on the disposition of endowment fund investments are treated, in accordance with state law, as endowment income, rather than as additions to endowment principal ("*corpus*").

Contributions and bequests. Contributions, including unconditional pledges (at their estimated net realizable value), are recognized as income in the period received or unconditionally promised. Bequests are recognized at the time the Organization's right to them is established by a court, and the proceeds are subject to reasonable estimation.

Donations and bequests received with donor stipulations as to their intended use are reported in the statement of activities as restricted support. Temporarily restricted net assets are reclassified as unrestricted when used or available for unrestricted use in accordance the donors' stipulations. Donations of equipment or other long-lived assets are classified as unrestricted, and restrictions on the use of cash donations for the purchase thereof are considered met when the assets are purchased, unless donor-imposed restrictions require that the assets be used or maintained by the Organization for a specified period.

The foregoing notwithstanding, pledges and bequests that relate to agency transactions are not recognized as such until paid (or non-cash assets transferred) to the Organization.

Non-cash ("in-kind") gifts of goods or services (which have not been material except for certain investment securities donated in prior years) are recorded as contributions at their estimated fair value at the date of receipt, except for donated services that do not meet the recognition criteria in Statement of Financial Accounting Standards No. 116, *Accounting for Contributions Received and Contributions Made*, including a substantial number of volunteer hours donated by individuals in the Organization's program activities and its fundraising campaigns.

Investment return includes interest, dividends and all realized and unrealized investment gains and losses. It is classified as unrestricted, except if otherwise specified by the donor of the invested funds.

Functional expenses. Expenses are allocated functionally to program and supporting activities, in part, on the basis of estimates by management. Costs associated with activities that include fundraising appeals and allocated to other activities have not been material.

As required by FASB Statement 117, *Financial Statements of Not-for-Profit Organizations*, all expenses are charged in the statement of activities to unrestricted net assets, regardless of how funded. Temporarily restricted net assets are then reclassified when available for unrestricted use as a result of compliance with or expiration of the related restriction.

Grant awards expense. Research grant expense (Note 4) is viewed by the Organization as compensation to scientific researchers for services and, therefore, the grants are treated as exchange transactions, and related expense is recognized over the grant period as earned by the "grantees."

IMAGINARY DISEASES FOUNDATION
NOTES TO FINANCIAL STATEMENTS (CONTINUED)

Year ended June 30, 1999

1. Description of operations and summary of accounting policies (continued):

Furniture, equipment and leasehold improvements. Expenditures for furniture, equipment and leasehold improvements are capitalized at cost or, for donated assets, fair value at the time of donation. Depreciation, including amortization of leasehold improvements, is provided on a straight-line basis over the estimated useful lives of the related assets.

2. Pledges

Pledges receivable at June 30, 1999, including bequests mature or are expected to be collected as follows:

Year ending June 30:	
2000	$ 571,518
2001	156,200
2002	79,630
	807,348
Less:	
Unamortized discount to estimated net present value	(27,120)
Allowance for doubtful collections	(100,000)
	$ 680,228

In addition, the Organization has conditional pledges totaling $350,000 that are not included in the accounts. Collection of the conditional pledges is dependent upon the Organization's ability to obtain matching gifts before June 30, 2001.

3. Investments and investment return:

As of June 30, 1999, the Organization's investments consisted of:

U.S. Treasury securities	$ 48,150
Corporate marketable securities:	
Equity instruments	207,622
Debt instruments	25,000
Time deposits	40,000
	$ 320,772

Management believes there are no significant concentrations of market risk in the Organization's investment portfolio.

Reported investment return for the year consists of:

Interest income	$ 33,166
Net unrealized investment gains	36,214
Dividends and net realized investment gains	17,817
	$ 87,197

4. Commitments:

Grant awards. The Organization enters into commitments, usually annually, to award scientific research and patient care grants. Research grants are awarded after review by the Organization's Medical Review Committee and approval by its Board of Trustees. Subject to an annual review and reapproval process, these grants generally cover a period of one to three years.

Subject to the grantees' meeting the applicable terms and conditions timely, grants awarded to date will become payable as follows:

Year ending June 30:	
2000	$ 692,595
2001	463,178
2002	94,100
	$1,249,873

Except as previously provided for by restricted gifts (Note 5), the Organization's ability to meet these grant commitments may be dependent on future contributions to be received.

Lease. The Organization leases its office facilities under an operating lease expiring in 2004. Base monthly rental payments are scheduled to increase by 4% annually. In addition, the Organization pays a *pro-rata* share of real estate taxes and other operating expenses. Obligations for deferred rent result from recognition of rent expense on a straight-line basis over the lease period.

Minimum rental payments due under the lease are:

Year ending June 30:	
2000	$ 127,166
2001	133,524
2002	138,835
2003	144,420
2004	123,150

100

Year ended June 30, 1999

4. Commitments (continued):

Lease (continued). Rent expense under the lease, excluding parking fees, amounted to $125,775 for the year ended June 30, 1999.

5. Restricted net assets:

As of June 30, 1999, net assets are temporarily restricted for the following purposes:

Research	$1,698,032*
Other programs	90,824
Other	60,000
	$1,848,856

---

* Of this amount, $236,000 is specifically linked to grant awards scheduled for payment during the year ending June 30, 2000, and the remainder is undesignated.

Permanently restricted net assets consist of endowment principal, the income from which is classified, as earned, as an increase in net assets temporarily restricted for research purposes.

6. Reconciliation of change in net assets to net cash provided by operations:

Change in net assets	$	919,358
Contributions received of marketable securities	(	5,000)
Net unrealized investment gains	(	36,214)
Depreciation		40,418
Bad debts expense		10,000
Decrease in pledges receivable		234,267
Increase in grants payable		146,954
Increase in accounts payable and accrued expenses		1,491
Increase in agency obligations		20,000
Decrease in deferred rent obligations	(	14,938)
Other		12,318
Net cash provided by operations		$1,328,654

101

APPENDIX B: GLOSSARY

This glossary is limited primarily to terms that have specific usage or applicability in the not-for-profit environment and important terms of general applicability that nonaccountants may not be sufficiently familiar with to properly understand the text.

- **Accrual basis of accounting** — The accounting practice of recognizing revenues when earned and expenses when related obligations have been incurred. Although several variations have been used, the opposite alternative is called the "cash basis" of accounting in which revenues are recognized only when cash (or other assets) have been received and expenses only when paid. Only accrual basis accounting is consistent with generally accepted accounting principles (GAAP).

- **Agency transaction** — A transfer of funds (sometimes called a "custodian" transaction) to an organization acting as an agent or intermediary under direction from the transferor to remit the funds to a designated third party recipient.

- **Agency obligation** — A liability arising from an agency transaction or group of agency transactions that is discharged only when the funds received by the intermediary organization are remitted, in turn, to the intended ultimate recipient.

- **Board-designated funds** — Unrestricted net assets subject to self-imposed limits by action of the governing board. Board-designated net funds may be treated as "quasi-endowments" with the *corpus* or income earned thereon earmarked for future programs, investments, contingencies, purchase or construction of buildings or improvements, or other specified uses.

- **Capital assets** — Long-lived assets, such as land and buildings, art and library collections, and furniture and equipment, or improvements thereto.

- **Capital budget** — a budget specifically for the acquisition and disposition of capital assets.

- **Capital expenditures** — Expenditures of cash or other resources to acquire capital assets.

- **Capital project** — a group of capital expenditures (or planned capital expenditures) related by a common purpose.

- **Capitalization policy** — A policy adopted by an organization defining the minimum dollar value of an expenditure for a property acquisition or improvement that is to be recorded on its books as an asset (capitalized), rather than charged to expense.

- **Cash** — Generally, coin, currency and checks. Sometimes used to refer to balance on deposit in banks and subject to withdrawal on demand.

- **Cash basis of accounting** — see "accrual basis of accounting."

- **Cash equivalents** — Highly liquid, short term investments, such as in "money market" funds, that are, in substance, like cash on deposit.

- **Collective (or common) trust funds** — Trust arrangements with banks, insurance companies or other financial institutions that involve pooled funds of several investors with similar investment objectives.

- **Conditional promise to give** — A pledge or promise to give that binds the donor only following the occurrence of a specified future and uncertain event.

- **Contribution** — An unconditional transfer of cash or other assets to an entity (or a cancellation or assumption of its liabilities) in a voluntary, nonreciprocal transfer by another person or entity other than an owner.

- *Corpus* — See "endowment *corpus*."

- **Custodian transaction** — see "agency transaction."

- **Defined benefit plan** — An employee retirement plan designed to produce a stated benefit upon retirement by requiring employer contributions determined based on actuarial computations.

- **Defined contribution plan** — An employee retirement plan that permits employer contributions (more or less, subject to any matching requirements) on a discretionary basis, resulting in retirement benefits that are determined based upon available assets at the time of withdrawal.

- **Development** — A term used by not-for-profit organizations to refer to the marketing/fundraising function.

- **Donor-imposed condition** — A donor stipulation that specifies a future and uncertain event whose occurrence or failure to occur releases the promissor from any obligation to transfer assets (or gives the promissor a right of return of assets it has transferred).

- **Employee leasing** — an arrangement in which a third party "lessor" provides personnel to perform employee services for an hourly fee, that includes reimbursement for the cost of all related payroll taxes and employee benefits, thus relieving the organization from the normal employer obligations to maintain a payroll, make payroll reports, and provide such benefits.

- **Endowment or endowment fund** — An established fund of cash, securities, or other assets to provide income for the maintenance of a not-for-profit organization or furtherance of its programs.

- **Endowment *corpus*** — The principal amount of an endowment fund that must be maintained over a specified period or in perpetuity.

- **Endowment income** — The portion of an endowment fund that is available to be spent for the donor-designated purpose of the endowment.

- **Exchange transaction** — A transaction in which cash, financial instruments, property, goods or services of equal value (or presumed equal value) are exchanged for the mutual benefit of the parties.

- **Federated campaign** — A fundraising campaign, usually conducted in the workplace, by an organization that allocates the proceeds thereof to a number of other qualifying organizations for expenditure in their programs and supporting activities.

- **Fiduciary** — A person or body of persons (for example, a board or committee) in a special relationship to others that constitutes a position of extraordinary trust and confidence and a duty to act in good faith.

- **Financial statements** — A group of related presentations of financial information, including accompanying disclosures, derived from accounting records and intended to communicate an entity's economic resources or obligations at a point in time (often called financial position or financial condition) or the changes therein for a period of time in conformity with GAAP (or another comprehensive basis of accounting). Typical financial statements of not-for-profit organizations (illustrated in *APPENDIX A* of this **HANDBOOK**) include:

  a. Statement of financial position
  b. Statement of activities
  c. Statement of cash flows
  d. Statement of functional expenses (usually presented only by voluntary health and welfare organizations)

- **Functional classification** — A method of grouping expenses according to the purpose for which costs are incurred, rather than their nature.

- **Fund accounting** — A bookkeeping technique or system commonly used by governmental agencies and not-for-profit organizations that establishes and maintains separate funds, each consisting of a self-balancing set of asset, liability, and net asset (fund balance) accounts, and appropriate related revenue, expense and fund transfer accounts. Fund accounting provides accountability for assets whose use is limited either by law or regulation, contract or other obligation, for example, by donor restriction or by federal agencies, other grantors, or the organization's own governing board.

- **Generally accepted accounting principles (GAAP)** — A technical accounting term that encompasses the conventions, rules, and procedures that define acceptable accounting practices for general external financial reporting purposes. GAAP includes accounting principles that are consistent with various levels of authoritative accounting standards and, in the absence of such standards, widely used industry practices and scholarly writings.

- **Gross receipts** — (for purposes of the federal Form 990 filing requirements) an organization's total gross revenues, without reduction for any costs but excluding any amounts received in agency transactions on behalf of others. For organizations reporting on the accrual basis of accounting, "gross receipts" would include accrued pledges receivable, net of an allowance for uncollectible pledges.

- **Imprest fund** — A bank account or petty cash fund with a fixed balance that is periodically restored through reimbursement as needed.

- **In-kind gift** — A non-cash contribution of goods, services or property.

- **Joint costs** — Costs incurred for fundraising activity that also benefits another purpose, usually program but sometimes management and general.

- **"Lockbox" service** — A service offered by banks that enables donors to mail checks directly to an entity's bank account for immediate deposit.

- **Misappropriation** — The unauthorized and fraudulent removal or defalcation of cash or other resources.

- **Natural classification** — A method of grouping expenses according to their nature, rather than the purpose for which costs are incurred.

- **Net assets** — The excess of recorded asset values over liabilities in total or in any given fund, group of funds or category.

- **Nonreciprocal transfer** — A transaction in which an entity incurs a liability or transfers cash or other resource to another entity (or receives an asset or cancellation of a liability) without directly receiving (or giving) value in consideration (as in an exchange transaction), for example, a contribution.

- **Not-for-profit organization** — Philanthropic, charitable or social welfare institutions and other organizations that enhance the fabric of American society, and are neither business (often called "for-profit") nor government. These organizations are often managed and staffed mostly by volunteers, and they possess the following additional characteristics in varying degrees that distinguish them from business enterprises: (a) contributions of significant amounts from resource providers who do not expect commensurate or proportionate pecuniary return, (b) operating purposes other than to provide goods or services at a profit, and (c) absence of traditional ownership interests.

- **Permanent restriction** — A donor-imposed restriction that stipulates that resources be maintained permanently but permits the organization to use up or expend part or all of the income (or other economic benefits) derived from the donated assets.

- **Planned giving** — A type of fundraising campaign that solicits relatively large, future gifts as part of a donor's overall estate planning, for example from insurance proceeds, bequests or trusts.

- **Pledge**— A common, non-technical term used for a promise to give.

- **Program or program activity** — An activity or group of activities that provide goods or services to beneficiaries in furtherance of an organization's mission or purpose.

- **Promise to give** — A written or oral agreement to contribute cash or other assets to another entity (commonly called a "pledge"). A promise to give may be either conditional or unconditional.

- **Reserves** — (as used in this **HANDBOOK**) Net assets held in excess of current operating needs, sometimes for a designated purpose.

- **Quasi-endowments** — See board designated net assets.

- **Special event** — An event, usually providing some benefit to participants, for example, dinner or entertainment, held primarily for fundraising purposes.

- **Split-interest agreement** — Trust or other arrangements initiated by donors under which not-for-profit organizations receive benefits that are shared with either the donor or third party beneficiaries. These gifts include lead interests and remainder interests, for example, charitable remainder trust, annuity gift, and annuity trust.

- **Strategic planning** — a long-range planning process that is based on the development of clear, often quantifiable, goals, broad strategies and specific action plans for the achievement thereof, and the periodic measurement and monitoring of performance progress and reconsideration of their continuing applicability

- **Supporting activities** — Any of a group of related services or activities that support the organization and enable it to function and conduct program activities, usually classified either as "management and general" or "fundraising" activities.

- **"Sweep" services** — A cash management service offered by banks and other financial institutions that automatically "sweeps" uninvested funds periodically from noninterest-bearing accounts to interest-bearing accounts (and *vice versa*), as needed

- **Temporary restriction** — A donor-imposed restriction that permits the donee organization to use up or expend the donated assets as specified and is satisfied either by the passage of time or by actions of the organization.

- **Unconditional promise to give** — A pledge or promise to give that depends only on passage of time or demand by the promisee for performance.

- **Variance power** — The unilateral ability (*i.e.*, without approval of donor, beneficiary or other interested party) to redirect a donor's gift (rather than to return it to the donor) in circumstances when it is judged either impossible or impractical to comply with the donor's wishes, or not consistent with the charitable needs of the community served by the organization.

- **Voluntary health and welfare organization** — A not-for-profit, usually tax exempt , organization that is formed for the purpose of performing voluntary services primarily to solve societal health and welfare problems or provide other community services, and that derives its revenue primarily from voluntary contributions from the general public.

- **"Watchdog" organization** — A non-governmental organization whose purpose is to protect the interests of donors and other public constituents from improprieties committed by charitable organizations, for example, false and misleading fundraising claims or financial reporting, and other accountability deficiencies.

- **"Zero-based" budgeting** — A goal-oriented budgeting process that starts with a "blank page" and, therefore, is not unduly biased by the effects of prior history or experience.

APPENDIX C: SELECTED BIBLIOGRAPHY

As stated in its introduction, the material in this **HANDBOOK** has been limited to brief highlights of its many financial management topics to enhance its simplicity, readability and utility by volunteer treasurers with limited time to devote to their roles.

Because of its vast significance in the American culture, the number of books, periodicals, websites and other reference sources about financial management aspects of the not-for-profit segment of our society is virtually endless. However, for those who need to delve more deeply into one or more of these topics, the accompanying list of selected resources believed to be still available at the time of this writing has been assembled:

- Accountants for the Public Interest, *What a Difference Nonprofits Make: A Guide to Accounting Procedures* (Revised Third Edition). Washington, DC, 1995.

- Accountants for the Public Interest, *What a Difference Preparation Makes: A Guide to the Nonprofit Audit.* Washington, DC, 1992.

- Accountants for the Public Interest, *What a Difference Understanding Makes: Guides to Nonprofit Management.* Washington, DC, 1994.

- American Institute of Certified Public Accountants, Inc., Audit and Accounting Guide, *Not-for-Profit Organizations.* New York, NY, 1996.

- Andringa, Robert C., and Engstrom, Ted W., *Nonprofit Board Answer Book: Practical Guidelines for Board Members and Chief Executives.* Washington, DC: National Center for Nonprofit Boards, 1998.

- Bernstein, Philip, *Best Practices of Effective Nonprofit Organizations: A Practitioner's Guide.* New York, NY: The Foundation Center, 1997.

- Blazek, Jody, *Financial Planning for Nonprofit Organizations.* New York, NY: John Wiley & Sons, Inc., 1996.

- Block, Stephen R., *Perfect Nonprofit Boards: Myths, Paradoxes and Paradigms.* Needham Heights, MA: Simon & Schuster Custom Publishing, 1998.

- Bryce, Herrington J., *The Nonprofit Board's Role in Establishing Financial*

Policies. Washington, DC: National Center for Nonprofit Boards, 1996.

- Bryson, John M., *Strategic Planning for Public and Nonprofit Organizations: A Guide to Strengthening and Sustaining Organizational Achievement* (Revised Edition). San Francisco, CA: Jossey-Bass Publishers, 1995.

- Ciconte, Barbara Kushner, CFRE, and Jacob, Jeanne G., CFRE, *Fund Raising Basics*. Gaithersburg, MD: Aspen Publishers, Inc., 1997.

- Connors, Tracy Daniel, *The Volunteer Management Handbook*. New York, NY: John Wiley & Sons, Inc., 1995.

- Dalsimer, John Paul, *Understanding Nonprofit Financial Statements*. Washington, DC: National Center for Nonprofit Boards, 1996.

- DiLima, Sara Nell, and Johns, Lisa T., *Nonprofit Organization Management: Forms, Checklists & Guidelines*. Gaithersburg, MD: Aspen Publishers, Inc., 1997.

- Duca, Diane J., *Nonprofit Boards: Roles, Responsibilities and Performance*. New York, NY: John Wiley & Sons, Inc., 1996.

- Eadie, Douglas C., *Beyond Strategic Planning*. Washington, DC, National Center for Nonprofit Boards, 1993

- Edles, L. Peter, *Fundraising: Hands-on Tactics for Nonprofit Groups*. New York, NY: McGraw-Hill Inc., 1993.

- Freeman, David F., and the Council on Foundations, *The Handbook on Private Foundations* (Revised Edition). New York, NY: The Foundation Center, 1991.

- Fry, Robert P., Jr., *Creating and Using Investment Policies: A Guide for Nonprofit Boards*. Washington, DC: National Center for Nonprofit Boards, 1997.

- Fry, Robert P., Jr., *Nonprofit Investment Policies: Practical Steps for Growing Charitable Funds*. New York, NY: John Wiley & Sons, Inc., 1998.

- Gillis, John, *Board Member Manual*. Frederick, MD: Aspen Publishers, Inc., 1997.

- Gillis, John, Editor, *Nonprofit Personnel Policies*. Gaithersburg, MD: Aspen Publishers, Inc., 1998 (updated annually).

- Grace, Kay Sprinkel, *The Board's Role in Strategic Planning* (with audiotape). Washington, DC, National Center for Nonprofit Boards, 1996

- Gross, Malvern J.; Larkin, Richard F.; Bruttomesso, Roger S., and McNally, John J., *Financial and Accounting Guide for Not-for-Profit Organizations* (Fifth Edition). New York, NY: John Wiley & Sons, Inc., 1995.

- Hankin, Jo Ann; Seidner, Alan; and Zietlow, John, *Financial Management for Nonprofit Organizations.* New York, NY: John Wiley & Sons, Inc., 1998.

- Herman, Melanie L., and White, Leslie T., *Leaving Nothing to Chance: Achieving Board Accountability Through Risk Management.* Washington, DC: National Center for Nonprofit Boards and Nonprofit Risk Management Center, 1998.

- Herrington, Bryce, *Financial & Strategic Management for Nonprofit Organizations.* Englewood Cliffs, NJ: Prentice-Hall Inc., 1992.

- Holmgren, Norah, *The Finance Committee: The Fiscal Conscience of the Nonprofit Board.* Washington, DC: National Center for Nonprofit Boards, 1995.

- Hopkins, Bruce R., *The Law of Tax-Exempt Organizations* (Seventh Edition). New York, NY: John Wiley & Sons, Inc., 1998.

- Johnson, Sandra, *The Audit Committee.* Washington, DC: National Center for Nonprofit Boards, 1993.

- Lang, Andrew S., *Financial Responsibilities of the Nonprofit Board.* Washington, DC: National Center for Nonprofit Boards, 1998.

- Lang, Andrew S., CPA, Editor, *A Practical Guide to Nonprofit Financial Management.* Gaithersburg, MD: Aspen Publishers, Inc., 1995.

- Larkin, Richard F., and DiTimmaso, *Not-for-Profit Accounting Field Guide 1999-2000.* New York, NY: John Wiley & Sons, Inc., 1999.

- Levy, Barbara R., ACFRE, and Marion, Barbara, CFRE, *Successful Special Events.* Gaithersburg, MD: Aspen Publishers, Inc., 1997.

- Maddox, David, *Budgeting for Not-for-Profit Organizations.* New York, NY: John Wiley & Sons, Inc., 1999.

- National Health Council, Inc., *The Black Book: Standards of Accounting and*

Financial Reporting for Voluntary Health and Welfare Organizations (Fourth Edition). Dubuque, IA: Kendall/Hunt Publishing Company, 1998.

- O'Connell, Brian, *The Board Member's Book: Making a Difference in Voluntary Organizations* (Second Edition). New York, NY: The Foundation Center, 1993.

- Salamon, Lester, *America's Nonprofit Sector: A Primer* (Revised Edition). New York, NY: The Foundation Center, 1999.

- Smith, Bucklin & Associates, *The Complete Guide to Nonprofit Management*. New York, NY: 1994.

- Stevens, Craig R., CPA; Benson, Martha L., CPA; and Sorkin, Horton L., Ph.D.; Editors; *Nonprofit Controller's Manual* (1999 Edition). New York, NY: Warren, Gorham & Lamont/RIA Group, 1999.

- Stoesz, Edgar, and Raber, Chester, *Doing Good Better: How to be an Effective Board Member of a Nonprofit Organization*. Intercourse, PA: Good Books, 1997.

- Struck, Darla, *Fund Raising for Nonprofit Board Members*. Gaithersburg, MD: Aspen Publishers, Inc., 1995.

- Wolf, Thomas, *Managing a Nonprofit Organization*. New York, NY: Simon & Schuster, 1984, 1990.

Additional publications are listed, together with other useful information, at the following websites:

- Aspen Publishers, Inc. — www.aspenpub.com

- Catholic Charities Nonprofit Resources — www.ccsj.org/n-profit.html

- The Chronicle of Philanthropy — www.philanthropy.com

- The Foundation Center — www.fdncenter.org

- Internet Nonprofit Center — www.nonprofits.org

- John Wiley & Sons, Inc. — catalog.wiley.com/ss/.1998088722/index.cgi

- National Center for Nonprofit Boards — www.ncnb.org

- Nolo Press — nixwannabe.lanminds.com/category/business.html#NONCON

- The NonProfit Times — www.nptimes.com

APPENDIX D: TOPICAL INDEX
(Page references to illustrations are in italics)

D

defalcation, 13, 107
defined benefit plan, 86, 104
defined contribution plan, 86, 87, 105
development, 43, 105
disclosure requirements, 20, 24, 25, 29
donor database, 15
donor restrictions, 13, 15, 17, 20, 46, 78, 79, 81
donor's promises, 22
donor-imposed condition, 105
dual signatures, 14, 50
dues, 21, 22

E

employee leasing, 86, 105
Employee Manual Maker, 84
employer identification number (E.I.N.), 74
endowment funds, 24, 27, 46, 80, 81, 105
endowment income, 80, 105
endowment principle. *See corpus*
ethical code of conduct, 70, 83
exchange transaction, 20-22, 25, 105, 107
executive committee, 6
exemption application, 73
expenses, 19, 25, 34, 35, 106, 107

F

FASB. *See* Financial Accounting Standards Board
federal unemployment tax, 73
federated campaign, 46, 105
fiduciary, 3, 7, 9, 58, 59, 66, 67, 106
finance committee, 6, 10, 34, 59, 65, 71
Financial Accounting Standards Board (FASB), 4, 18-20, 22, 24-26, 30

financial reporting process, 7, 13, 17, 30, 69, 83
financial statement presentation, 18, 20
financial statements, 14, 26, 27, 30, 45, 65-70, *95-101*, 106
fraud, 13, 107
functional classification, 19, 27-29, 106
fund accounting, 19, 26, 27, 50, 79, 106
fund group, 26, 27
fundraising, 19, 25, 28-30, 33, 36, 40, 41, 43, 45-47, 58, 64, 77, 78, 83, 105, 107, 108, 109, 110
funds, 17, 26, 27, 43, 50, 59, 106, 107

G

GAAP. *See* generally accepted accounting principles (GAAP)
gambling winnings, 75
general journal, 18
general ledger, 18
generally accepted accounting principles (GAAP), 19, 20-27, 29, 30, 66, 68, 76, 103, 106
government grants, 47, 78
gross receipts, 74, 75, 107
group exemption, 74, 75, 78

H

human resource management policies, 83, 84

I

IMA. *See* Institute of Management Accountants
IMA "Standards of Ethical Conduct for Practitioners of Management Accounting and Financial Management," 83
imprest funds, 51, 53, 107

116

temporarily restricted net assets, 20,
 21, 24, 25, 27, 80, 81, 109
term endowments, 80
treasurer, 1, 5, 6, 7, 9-11, 13, 31, 33,
 45, 50, 52, 58, 59, 65, 69, 70, 71,
 73, 78, 79, 80, 89
trust departments, 64

U

UMIFA. *See* "Uniform Management
 of Institutional Funds Act"
unconditional promise to give, 55,
 108, 109
"Uniform Management of
 Institutional Funds Act"
 (UMIFA), 81
United Way. *See* United Way of
 America
United Way of America (UWA), 1, 2,
 3, 6, 7, 9, 46
unrelated business income, 73
unrestricted net assets, 20, 21, 24, 25,
 27, 80, 81
UWA. *See* United Way of America

V

variance power, 21, 109
voluntary health and welfare
 organizations, 19, 106, 109

W

"watchdog" organization, 3, 9, 17, 28,
 34, 45, 110
writeoffs, 22, 56

Y

"Y2K issue" or "millenium bug," 89

Z

"zero-based" budget, 35, 110

NOTES

NOTES

NOTES

NOTES

NOTES

ORDER FORM
(May be reproduced as needed)

If you would like to order additional copies of *The Volunteer Treasurer's Handbook: Financial Management Building Blocks for Not-for-Profit Organizations*, they may be obtained directly from the publisher for $19.95 each, plus 10% shipping and handling (and sales tax, if applicable), subject to the following discounts:

10 to 49 copies	10% off
50-99 copies	20% off
100+ copies	25% off

Please complete the following, and mail with your check (sorry, no telephone orders or credit cards), and any comments you may have about this **HANDBOOK**, to:

> *The Volunteer Treasurer's Handbook*
> ***PIERCY, BOWLER TAYLOR & KERN***, CPAs
> 6100 Elton Avenue, Suite 1000
> Las Vegas, NV 89107
>
> Allow 2 weeks for delivery.

QUANTITY REQUESTED

                                       X $19.95 ea.

1st subtotal	_____
add 10% S&H	_____
2nd subtotal	_____
less applicable discount	(_____)
3rd subtotal	_____
Nevada purchasers add 7¼ % sales tax *	_____
TOTAL REMITTANCE $	_____

SHIP TO:

Name of individual _____

Name of organization _____

Street address (or P.O. Box) _____

City, State, ZIP _____

---

*   Nevada tax-exempt organizations omit tax, and include copy of exemption certificate.